AF530330

Marriage and career both require selection. Your inclination and priorities effect the selection. When these two are combined with Vaastu and Feng Shui, there are infinite possibilities of success.

A logical and scientific study of how Vaastu and Feng Shui can bring happiness and prosperity in married life and bright future of the students, has been presented in this book.

Vaastu Shaastra and Feng Shui

Vaastu Guru Kuldeep Saluja

The much useful Series of 'Vaastu Shaastra and Feng Shui' by Kuldeep Saluja (Vaastu Guru) gives complete solution to all the problems which cause constant setback in one's life. This valuable series entails topics like Industry and Business, Flat and Office, Building and Construction, Wealth, Prosperity and Fame, Good Health, Marriage, Career, Interior Decoration and.Plot. This topics have been dealt in full detail to provide complete solutions to frequently asked questions.

Wealth, Prosperity & Fame... 75.00

Marriage, Career & Student... 75.00

Flat & Office... 75.00

Good Health... 75.00

Industry & Business... 75.00

Interior Decoration... 75.00

Building Construction... 75.00

Plot... 75.00

Books can be requisitioned by V.P.P. Postage charges will be Rs. 20/- per book. For orders of three books the postage will be free.

DIAMOND POCKET BOOKS (P.) Ltd.

X-30, Okhla Industrial Area, Phase-II, Phone : 011-41611861-5, Fax : 011-41611866
E-mail : sales@diamondpublication.com, Website : www.diamondpublication.com

VAASTU, FENG SHUI

Marriage & Career

Vaastu Guru

Kuldeep Saluja

FUSION BOOKS

ISBN - 81-8419-040-9

Publisher	:	**Fusion Books**
		X-30, Okhla Industrial Area,
		Phase-II, New Delhi-110020.
Phone	:	011-41611861
Fax	:	011-41611866
E-mail	:	sales@diamondpublication.com
Website	:	www.diamondpublication.com
Edition	:	2007

Vaastu, Feng Shui–*Marriage & Career*
By Vaastu Guru Kuldeep Saluja

DEDICATION

This book is dedicated to
my respected Parents
(Late) Sardar Tara Singh Ji Dhoul
and
(Late) Smt. Rampyari Dhoul.

PREFACE

Vaastushaastra is an old science. It is related to universal truth and not any religion or cult. After research for thousands of years our *rishi-munis* have made it useful for common people.

Vaastushaatra is very significant in today's lifestyle. In present times if anything goes wrong in the life of a person then, in addition to all other factors he also thinks about Vaastu defects at his residence and/or office. It is due to this increasing popularity of Vaastushaastra that every Tom, Dick and Harry is now *Vaastushaastri* these days. Interestingly you will find that some of them even do not know how to look at compass properly. These *Vaastushaastris* have created their own remedies to remove Vaastu defects, e.g. to plant *tulsi* in front of house, to tie a cow in front of house, to bury a pyramid in the earth or on the door, to put *'Yantra'* in copper plate, to put God's idol or Shri Yantra etc.

Vaastushaastra is a medium to take advantage of energy present in the nature by coordinating with the same. Nowadays Vaastushaastra has become a fashion and due to this it is practised more as a superstition and less on scientific basis.

I regularly write on Vaastu in the famous magazine *'Grihlaxmi'* and receive a lot of mail from my readers. I made up my mind to write on this science of construction (Building) after receiving my readers' mail. I wanted to help them to solve their Vaastu problems in a scientific way. I also wanted to remove their illusion, about Vaastu and to save them from the cheating done by many of the so-called *Vaastushaastris*.

I have studied books on Vaastu by learned *Vaastushaastris* like Sri B.N. Reddy, Sri Dronam Raju, Puranchandra Rao and

Sri R.G. Rao. This inspired me to write and unveil many mysteries of the subject. I am indebted to them.

I would like to extend my special thanks to Dr. Rashmi Ramdhoni, Associate Prof. Head of the Hindi Department, Mahatma Gandhi Institute, Mauritius, who translated my articles on Vaastu in French. These were published in the *"Week End"*, the main newspaper of Mauritius media.

I extend my thanks to Shri Sanjay Sharma for translating this work into English.

I am indebted to my wife Smt. Kuldeep Saluja, daughters-in-law, Sheetal and Rashmi, for their loving support.

Last but not the least, I extend my gratitude to Sri Narendra Kumar Varma (Publisher and Director, Diamond books) for his encouragement, which has enabled me to put my deep study and research in the form of this book.

–Kuldeep Saluja
Vaastu Guru

CONTENTS

UNIVERSAL VAASTUSHAASTRA AND FENG SHUI

Vaastushaastra and Feng shui both are old sciences of India and China to coordinate between buildings or shape of land, proportions and direction with the environment of their surroundings. Vaastu affects houses, shops, factories, schools, hospitals, *dharamshalas*, public offices, religious places, rivers, crematoria, casinos, bars, brothels etc. and even roads, squares, three roads, streets, towns, cities, i.e. everyplace on earth equally.

These days when somebody constructs his house he takes utmost care to decorate its outer and inner sides. He also takes care to get maximum comforts in the house, but he never seriously thinks whether his new house will provide him happiness, prosperity, fame, health and peace or not. If you are living in a place but do not get mental peace, good health, family is distressed and under pressure, you go through all types of troubles continuously. Do you think that there is any use in living in such a place?

Vaastushaastra was invented after continuous research by our *rishi–munis* to provide happy life and to save all of us from troubles of life in the world. The principles of Vaastushaastra are completely according to the principles of nature.

All the ancient palaces, temples and towns which were constructed as per the Vaastu principles are still shining, e.g. Tirupati Balaji Temple of Andhra Pradesh, Badrinath Temple, Maa Vaishnodevi Temple, Taj Mahal, Temples of Khajuraho, and Jaipur city etc. The buildings that were not constructed as per the Vaastu principles are nowhere to be seen now.

We can experience the examples of Vaastu around us. Sometimes we feel happy on entering the house of a friend and there is an inner feeling to go there again and again. On the other hand, in some other house the moment we enter a sort of suffocating feeling comes in our heart and we do not wish to go there again. Similarly, we find that a tenant in a certain house in our neighborhood succeeds in every field of life and then constructs a house of his own and shifts to the same, whereas there is a house wherein if anybody stays he is always in trouble. All the family members remain troubled financially, physically and mentally and one day they leave the house. Some people construct extravagant house with all the modern facilities and live there, but later on they die without any kids and that house is ruined. Many factory owners face labour problems, governmennt raids, accidents etc. in the initial stage itself and they finally close the same. On the other hand, there are examples of people who had humble beginnings, got success rapidly, increased their business manifold, became rich and lived a happy and prosperous life.

If a hut is constructed as per Vaastu then the residents do not face much trouble for their daily needs. The family progresses and gradually becomes prosperous. Opposite to this if a bungalow is not constructed as per Vaastu the residents of the same have to struggle even for daily needs, no matter how rich they are. They gradually lose their social status and prosperity. Their lives become miserable due to continuous physical, mental and financial problems. There are certain "Vaastu-defects", which are to be eradicated immediately as they start affecting very soon.

While applying Vaastu the importance is given to the house in which you live no matter whether you are an owner or a tenant or even it could be a temporary or permanent place of your stay. Vaastu is applicable everywhere. Suppose you are sailing in a boat and there is a hole at the bottom of the same, now it is almost certain that you will be drown but the fact that the boat owner is somebody else and you only boarded it to cross the river does not change its result.

The Vaastu consultant has to be especially sensitive towards two things– first, the needs of those living in the premises and second, the requirement of the same premises. It is because the house is for those who live in. An able Vaastu consultant is one who coordinates between the Vaastu principles and available resources of a premises.

THE INDIAN VAASTUSHAASTRA

The fundamentals of the Indian Vaastushaastra are five universal five elements, i.e. earth, water, fire, wind and sky. Our body and the whole universe are made up of these five elements.

Vaastu is basically to construct and decorate our house as per these five elements. Vaastu is a science which guides us to take maximum advantage of the magnetic effect present in earth and solar energy. It creates such an effect that by the use of positive and negative solar energy in right proportion we get happiness, peace, prosperity and fame. If you coordinate with three elements viz. earth, water and fire out of the five, the wind and sky are automatically coordinated.

THE CHINESE FENG SHUI AND VAASTUSHAASTRA

Feng Shui is Chinese Vaastushaastra. It is almost 5000 years old science of China. Its meaning is wind and water. In any building if there is right balance between these two then the positive energy is increased and it produces happiness, peace and prosperity. As per the Feng Shui principle, the fortune of a man is of three types:

1. **Fortune From Heaven** : The fortune, which the man gets from his past birth and deeds.
2. **Fortune Created by Man** : This is the fortune which the man creates by his deeds. It is also called his hard earned fortune.
3. **Fortune From Earth** : This is due to the shape, proportion, direction and environment of the house and office etc.

As per Feng Shui there are two types of energies in nature–one is positive and another is negative. The positive energy is called YIN and the negative YANG. Feng Shui coordinates between Yin and Yang in such a way that they are useful for human beings to get happiness, prosperity, mental peace and good health etc.

Yin & Yang

FORTUNE AND VAASTU

Nothing is superior to the fortune. If the fortune of a person is strong and Vaastu is bad even then he gets success but it's after hard work and struggle. If fortune and Vaastu both are strong the person gets success easily and without any struggle. The troubled time of a person passes easily if the fortune is weak and Vaastu is strong, but if fortune and Vaastu both are weak then it is very difficult for that person to cope with the bad times.

It is true that nobody can change the fortune by merely changing the directions but by doing so one can get a bit of relief too. People may say that if the fortune cannot be changed then why we should waste our time in Vaastu.

I would like to give you one example, suppose you fall ill then why do you visit to your doctor? Why don't you simply sit and wait to get well. If you are destined to get well, you will live. But you go to see your doctor and get proper medicines. Similarly, if due to weak fortune you are suffering from physical, mental and financial problems, then you can get some relief by Vaastu. Certainly, we can lead a happy life by just rearranging some things as per Vaastu.

FAITH AND VAASTU

All the civilizations of the world have their religious symbols. In India also we have *Swastika, Om, Shree, Panchgulak Hand,* 786, *Omkar* etc. People have faith in different types of *yantras* too e.g. 'Lakshmi Yantra', 'Shree Yantra', 'Kuber Yantra', 'Kaali Yantra' and 'Surya Yantra' etc.

Most of the intellectuals think that only superstitious and idle people wear amulet, *rudraksh*, rings and *yantras* etc. but on the contrary it is true wearing them is very useful. A research has been done by Prof. Richard Wisemen and his scholars of Heartfordshire University, England on the benefits of wearing rings and *rudraksh* etc. religious symbols. They claim to have found corrected destiny of people after wearing these symbols.

Certainly the use of religious symbols and *yantras* develops the positive thinking. People become optimistic about their future. The user of these symbols gets rid of disappointment and develops self-confidence. By the inspiration of self-confidence the person works hard to get success.

These religious symbols are in frequent use to eradicate Vaastu defects in our country. 'Shri Yantra', 'Swastik yantra', 'Vaastu defects eradication Yantra', 'Sawastika', 'Pyramid', 'Siddha Ganapati' and 'Panchmukhi Hanuman' etc. are some of the religious symbols in use. Some Chinese religious symbols such as laughing Buddha, double happiness symbol, Fuk-Luk and Sau, three legged frog and lucky coin are also in use in addition to the Indian religious symbols. These symbols whether proved or not, are not very much useful to eradicate Vaastu defects. When a doctor treats some serious ailment of a patient he usually prescribes some vitamins etc. in addition to the actual medicines. These religious symbols are like vitamin tablets, which do not eradicate Vaastu defects.

As vitamin tablets cannot eradicate a disease, similarly, Vaastu defects also cannot be corrected by using religious symbols. We have to make alterations and modifications in the building to eradicate significant Vaastu defects.

We can explain it by an example, suppose in a building the main gate is in the corner of the "south west zone" and there is an underground water tank, well or bore-well near that main gate, then there is maximum possibility of unnatural death of one of the male family members. If you want to correct this Vaastu defect by using any of the religious symbols, it will definitely not work. This Vaastu defect can only be corrected by closing this gate and constructing a new gate in west of the north-west and the underground water source has also to be closed by soil filling.

We can understand the significance of the removal of Vaastu defect by the following example. If we put zero after 1 then it becomes 10. Again by putting one more zero we can make it 100. So by putting one zero we can increase the value of a digit ten times. But if the digit 1 is not there then there is no value of a zero. So all the changes made in a building as per Vaastu are like a digit if we put religious symbols they increase the effect of changes made, but symbol alone can not be effective.

VAASTUSHAASTRA IS A SCIENCE

The principles of Vaastushaastra are fully scientific. We can prove it by analyzing some of them.

1. **Water in North-East Zone :** If the water source is in the north-east zone then all the bacteria etc. present in the water are destroyed by morning sun rays. This fact is also confirmed by science.
2. **Courtyard in the East:** It is recommended to get sunbath and maximum exposure to sun rays in the morning. It is supposed to be very useful for health.
3. **Tree in the East:** Big trees are not to be grown in the east of the house as they obstruct the positive morning sun rays from entering the house.
4. **Kitchen in the South-East Zone:** If the kitchen of the house is in the south-east zone the morning sun rays enter the kitchen from east, which destroy bacteria and germs in food.
5. **High and Thick Walls in the West:** The morning sun rays are useful. They give advantage but when the sun is in the west, at the time of noon, the sun rays are harmful. Vaastushaastra suggests us to construct high and thick walls in the south-west to protect us from these harmful sun rays.
6. **Head in South Direction While Sleeping:** Our head works as the North Pole and legs as the South Pole. If we keep our head in north direction while sleeping, then there will be a distraction due to the North Pole of the earth.

This will create a tension and disturb sleep. That's why Vaastushaastra suggests us to keep our head in south while sleeping. This will give us sound sleep and good health.

Thus many scientific logics prove the principles of Vaastushaastra. Hence we should remove the Vaastu defects scientifically only. Whenever there is a Vaastu defect it cannot be removed or corrected by any charm, *puja* or religious symbol. If the Vaastu of a temple is defective then people are not attracted towards the same while the God himself sits in the temple.

Vaastushaastra and Feng Shui help us in improving every field of the life. Removal of Vaastu defects of the house and office, etc. with the help of Vaastushaastra and Feng Shui produces wonderful results. That's why this centuries old oriental science is fast becoming popular in the West too.

IMPROTANCE OF THE SUN IN VAASTU

The whole universe gets life from the sun. In fact, the sun is the base of the universe. East direction is the way through which we get the positive energy of the sun. That is why east and north are two very significant directions as per Vaastu. The energy of the sun enters any house or building from north-east zone only and the space energy also enters the same way. A special energy region is produced by the fusion of these two energies. This gives positive results to the inhabitants.

Man is aware of vital power of the sun. From the beginning various civilizations have worshipped the sun. This proves vital importance of the sun.

The morning sun rays possess many advantageous things– this has been proved by science also. Our skins absorb vitamin D from these sun rays. The white sun rays actually consist of seven colours i.e. violet, indigo, blue, green, yellow, orange and red. All these colours affect our health. Colour and naturopathy use sun rays. These sun rays destroy germs and bacteria.

The morning sun rays are best due to their less temperature and more light. That's why the Vaastushaastra recommends keeping more space, doors and windows in the east so that more and more sun rays enter the house and the courtyard. This destroys the bacteria and germs and produces healthy environment for a healthy life. Good health is the biggest wealth.

REMEDIES OF VAASTUSHAASTRA AND FENG SHUI AND THEIR LIMITATIONS

There are various points and effective remedies to remove Vaastu defects of any building in the Indian Vaastushaastra. Most of these remedies require demolition of certain construction and then new construction as per Vaastu. For example a toilet in the north-east zone is inauspicious as per Vaastu. Hence it is removed from there and constructed at some other appropriate place. If bore well or other underground water source is not in the north-east zone then it is fully closed and constructed in the north-east zone.

Chinese Vaastushaastra– Feng Shui– says that if there is a problem there is a remedy. Feng Shui uses some external and internal remedies to remove some small Vaastu defects. The following list gives an idea about the things used to remove Vaastu defects by Feng Shui.

Light and things reflect light, living things, comfortable sounds, moving things, mechanical things, water, plants and colours etc.

PYRAMID AND VAASTU

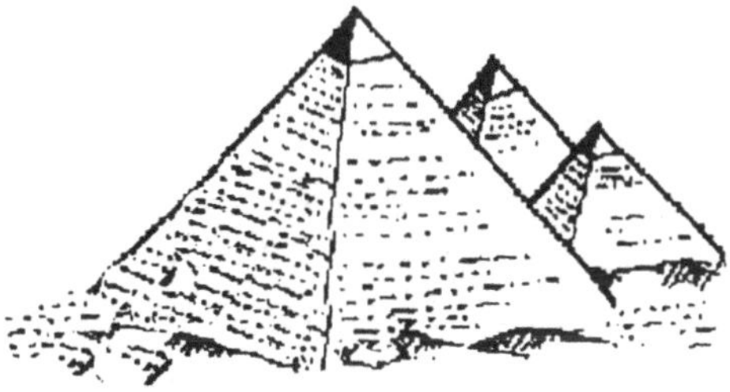

The pyramids are tombs of the Pharaohs or kenps of ancient Egypt on the banks of the Nile River. These are about four thousand years old. These were constructed as per Vaastu in a straight line of the Pole Star in the sky in north direction. The pyramid structures are really unique example of Vaastu and medicinal specialty. Taking the inspiration from the pyramids of Egypt many experiments were performed in various countries of the world. In one such experiment a dead body was kept in the pyramid and amazingly the body did not decay. Mr. Bowis, a French investigator, was amazed to find that inside the pyramid when a rat or cat died no bad smell was produced. The body mummified, dried and did not decay. He could not find any plausible explanation for this whole phenomenon. After a lot of thinking he concluded that this might be due to the shape of the pyramid. For the confirmation of this he prepared a small pyramid and put a dead cat in the same. He was surprised to find that the cat did not decay and was mummified. He then experimented with other perishable things like vegetables and milk.

He found that these things remained fresh for about a week. He kept rubbish beneath the pyramid and found that this too dried without any bad smell. This gave birth to a new science that the geometrical shapes are deeply related to life energies. Now Bowis suggests that all the hospitals should be constructed in the pyramid shape so that the patients get well soon. Many experiments have been done on this concept. If a wound is kept inside the pyramid shape it heals faster. Similarly toothache, headache etc. are relieved faster when kept beneath the pyramid shape.

Pyramid word consist of a Greek word 'Pyre' = fire and 'Mid' = centre. So the meaning of the word is that pyramid is a place that has fire (energy) at its centre. It is this energy that keeps things fresh inside it. For centuries temples, mosques, churches, *gurudwaras*, Bodh *matts* etc. have been constructed with upper shape as a dome, which is a kind of pyramid only. We get fresh air and peace if we sit beneath these dome shaped structures. It gives us mental happiness and concentration due to a special energy that flows through this pyramid (dome) shape. In short, we can say that a pyramid is an equipment to store energy. Pyramids are useful in medicine and meditation but they are not useful to remove Vaastu defects.

In Egypt also, where pyramids were invented, they were used to keep dead bodies safe. The world renowned Feng Shui practitioner, Lilian Too, has also described the misuse of the pyramids in Vaastu defects. In China, from where Feng Shui originated, pyramids are not used to remove Vaastu defects.

Note: Please read *"Vaastu & Feng Shui for Better Health"* by the same author to know the misuse of pyramid in removing Vaastu defects.

SHREE YANTRA AND VAASTU

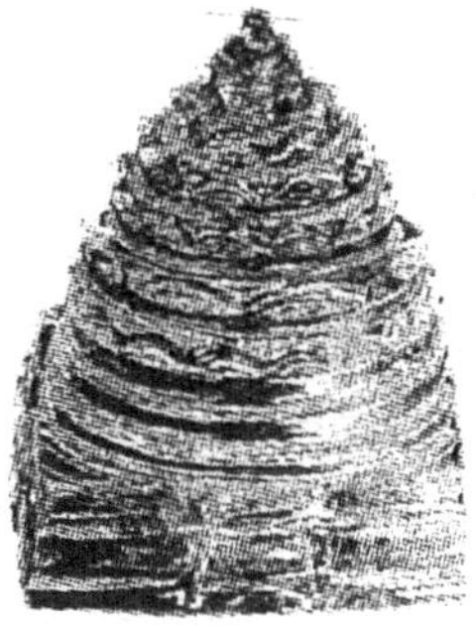

Shree Yantra has religious importance no matter whether proved or not. It may be made up of quartz or any other metal but has no use in removal of Vaastu defects. Here I want to clear one thing that the quartz Shree Yantra may be religiously important but quartz circles have their own use in removal of Vaastu defects. The quartz circle works as a prism, reflects light which has a scientific basis. These circles are used to attract more natural light through window, when placed in front of window panes. Cuts of these circles reflect more light to make the place full of energy.

Note: To know the misuse of the Shree Yantra in detail, please read *"Vaastu & Feng Shui for Happiness & Prosperity"* by the same author.

DETERMINATION OF DIRECTION IN VAASTUSHAASTRA AND FENG SHUI

A magnetic compass is used to determine the directions in the Indian Vaastushaastra. While determining the Vaastu disposition of a building the magnetic compass is kept at the centre of the building. The Vaastu defect of the building can only be removed by this direction determination.

The Chinese Feng Shui uses two methods. First is the use of "Luo Pan", the Chinese compass. Auspicious and inauspicious directions are determined on the basis of the date of birth in this method. The second method is based on magic square called – Pa Kua. Every Vaastu is divided into eight parts in it based on the main gate of the building or the door of the room. In this method, the north direction is always there where the gate is.

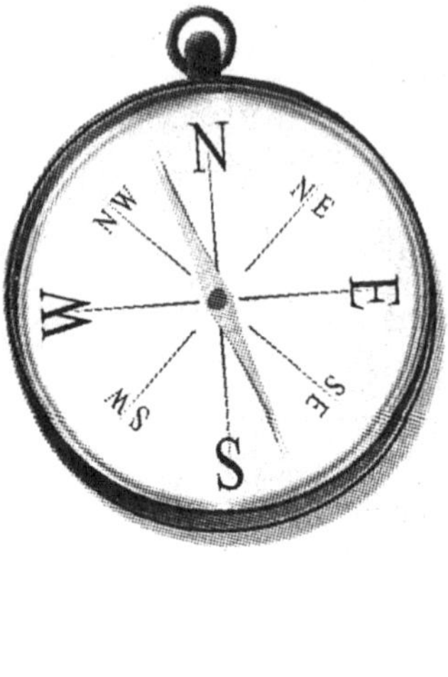

Chinese Compass Luo Pan

No compass is used in the Pa Kua method. Many small problems could be removed by just applying this method. This method is currently very popular in India.

Nine Planets Affecting Eight Directions

As per the Indian Vaastushaastra the nine planets present in our solar system affect all the eight directions of a plot or building. Every planet represents one direction as below:

DIRECTION PLANET

ENGLISH	HINDI	ENGLISH	HINDI
East	*Purva*	Sun	*Surya*
South	*Dakshin*	Mars	*Mangal*
West	*Paschim*	Saturn	*Shani*
North	*Uttar*	Mercury	*Budh*
South-East	*Agneya*	Venus	*Shukr*
South-West	*Nairitya*	Rahu	*Rahu*
North-West	*Vayavya*	Moon	*Chandrma*
North- East	*Ishaan*	Jupiter/Ketu	*Guru/Ketu*

DIRECTIONS AND ANGLES AS PER VAASTUSHAASTRA

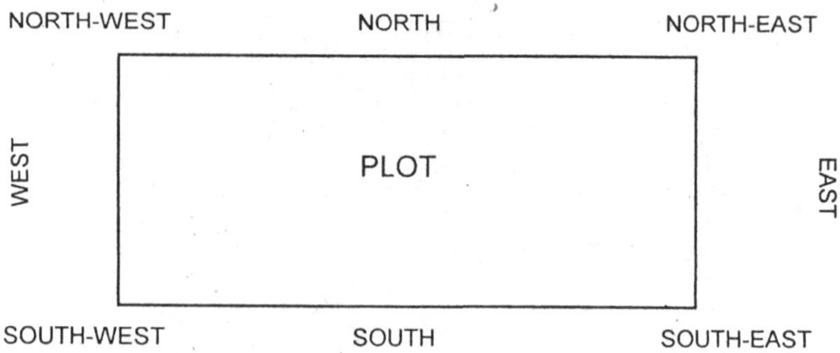

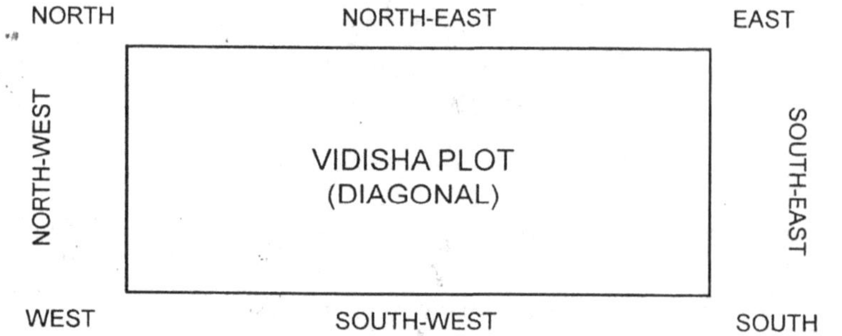

"A plot which has directions at the corners is called a "VIDISHA PLOT(DIAGONAL)".

FOUR DIRECTIONS

East *Purva* – Direction of sunrise.
West *Pashchim* – Direction of sunset.
North *Uttar* – Direction of the North Pole.
South *Dakshina* – Direction of the South Pole.

FOUR ANGLES

North-East *Ishaan* – Direction in between north and east.
South-East *Agneya* – Direction in between east and south.
South-West *Nairutya* – Direction in between west and south.
North-West *Vayavya* – Direction in between west and north.

DIVISION OF PLOT

Division of plot in eight parts as per Vaastu.

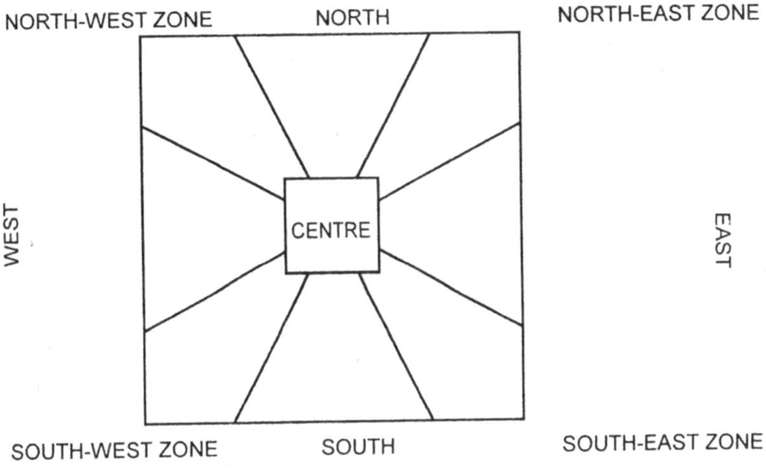

Division of a VIDISHA (Diagonal) plot as per Vaastu

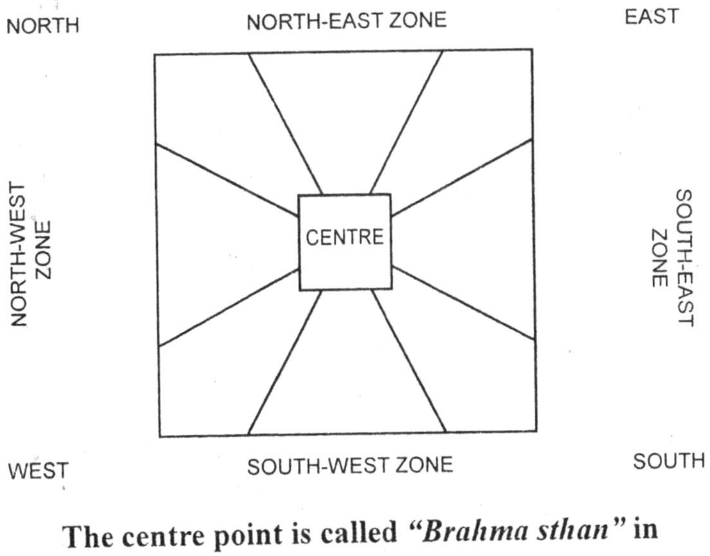

The centre point is called *"Brahma sthan"* in Vaastushaastra.

DIVISION OF VAASTU IN EIGHT PARTS AS PER FENG SHUI

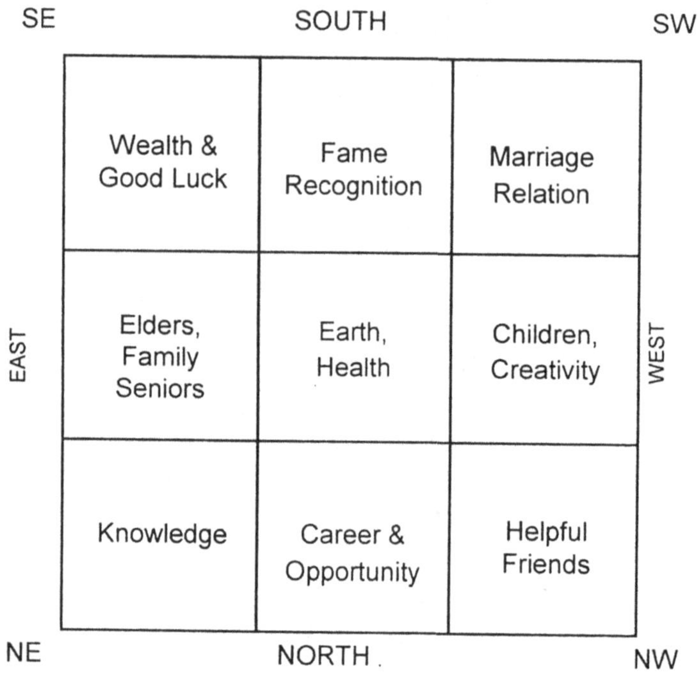

Main gate could be anywhere in this direction.

As per the magic square Pa-kua system of Feng Shui, a plot/building/room can be divided into eight parts. The direction of the main gate is always north.

MARRIAGE – VAASTU & FENG SHUI

It is a big problem to find proper match for youngsters reaching the age of the marriage, in every community of India. That's why, many of them remain unmarried. Parents are generally perplexed in finding proper match for their able and educated children. Sometimes the marriage relationship is broken, when in progress and many times it is broken after it is fixed. Nobody understands the reason behind this. In addition to other reasons, one very significant reason behind this is the Vaastu defect of the building, where they live.

Hong Kong based Varma family was much perplexed for the marriage of their promising good natured and beautiful daughter. The marriage could not be finalized due to one or another reason even after selecting proper match for her. I found the room of their daughter in the southwest zone and its door in the south of the southwest zone, when visited their house. A single bed was with the wall of east direction. All these were significant Vaastu defects. They shifted their daughter in a room in the northwest zone, on my advice. Luckily the door of this room was also in the west of the northwest zone. A double bed, which could be used from east, west and north, was put along with the wall in the south direction of the room. She was married to the son of a prestigious Khanna family of London, within two months of this change.

The marriage of the children can be fixed with proper match in time, if the parents follow the principles of Vaasushaastra and Feng Shui, while constructing their houses and making corrections:

- The plot on which your house is situated should be of rectangular or square shape for good fortune. It should not be of irregular shape. The southwest zone of the plot should be of 90 degree. There must be ample open space in the north and east directions. Family members live happy lives and have affection for each other in such houses.

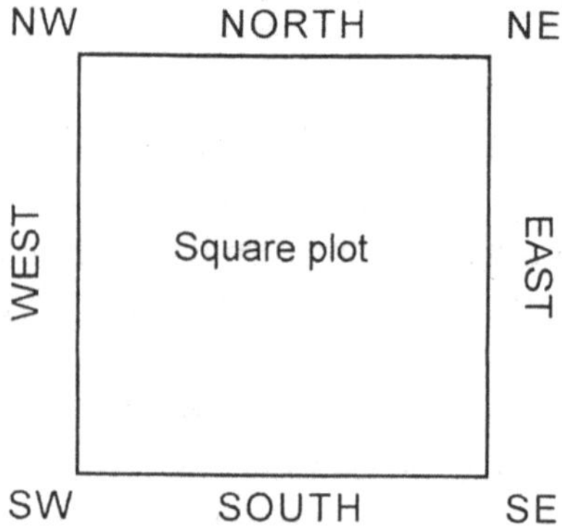

Square plot

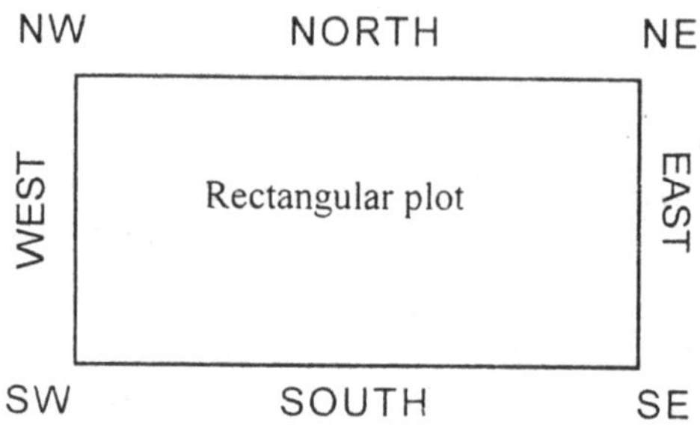

Rectangular plot

- Construct or purchase your house in such a place which has deep pits, ponds and river in the north and east and higher mounds and hillocks in the south and west. Such a house will be a boon for you.

- Never construct or purchase house that has higher buildings, hillocks, rocks or big trees, like *pipal* and banyan tree etc. to its north and east directions. In addition to this, the house with deep pits, ponds and rivers in the southwest zone also creates problems in the married life.
- House must be constructed in rectangular or square shape, after leaving ample space in the north and east directions for good fortune. Care must be taken to construct all the rooms with right angles. One will lead a happy and grand life in such a house constructed as per Vaastu.

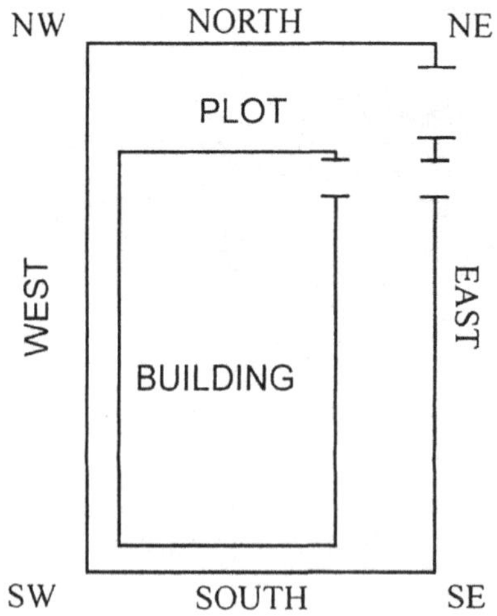

Ideal position of the house on the plot

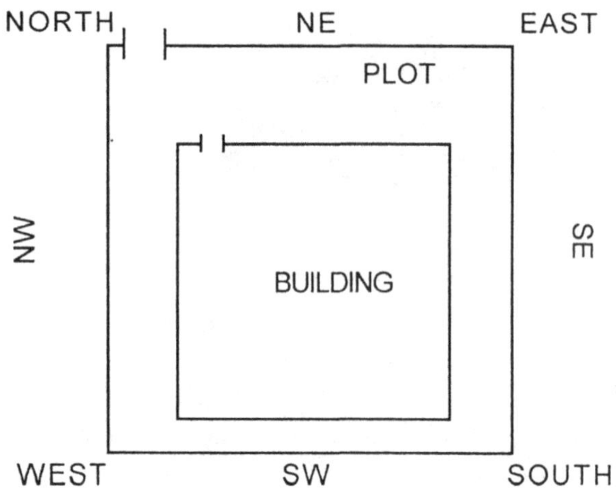

Ideal position of the house on the Vidisha plot

- Special care must be taken of the northeast zone while carrying out the construction of the house, as this is a very significant zone of all the eight directions. Cut, depressed or round part of the building or wall of the building in this zone is very inauspicious. This defect affects the marriageable person of the house also. The house must be made right-angled in this zone to remove this defect. This will save from inauspicious effects of the same.

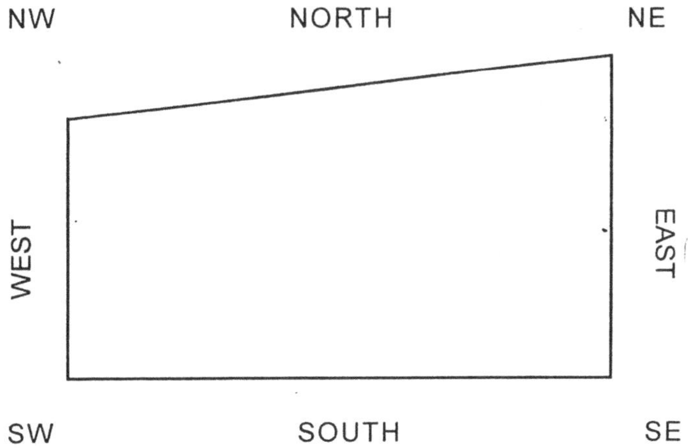

Building protruded in the north of the northeast zone

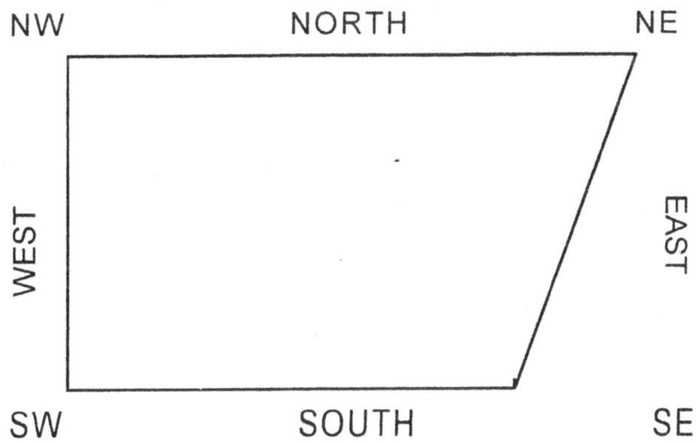

Building protruded in the east of the northeast zone

- The east, north and northeast zone of the house should be lower than the west, south and southwest for good fortune. Higher northeast zone invites bad luck and creates problems in finding life partner too.

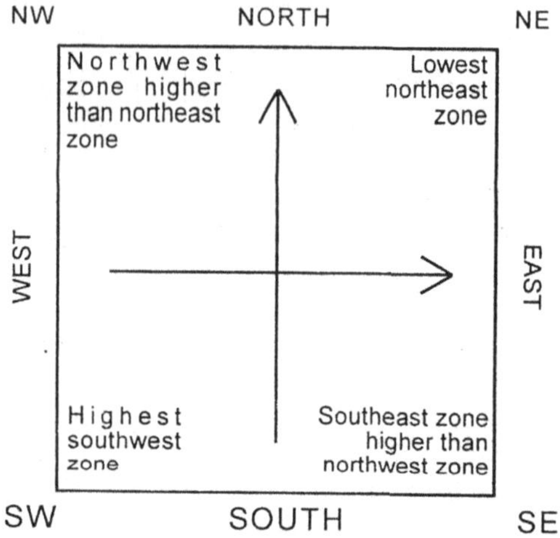

Highness & Lowness of the Plot as per Vaastu

- It is auspicious to have underground water tank, well or bore-well in the east, north or northeast zone of the house. This brings progress and happiness for children. They are married in time and the family is multiplied. These produce opposite results, if present in any other direction.

- The doors of the rooms of the marriageable persons in the family should be kept as per the indications in the figure. If it is not so, then they face a lot of troubles in getting married.

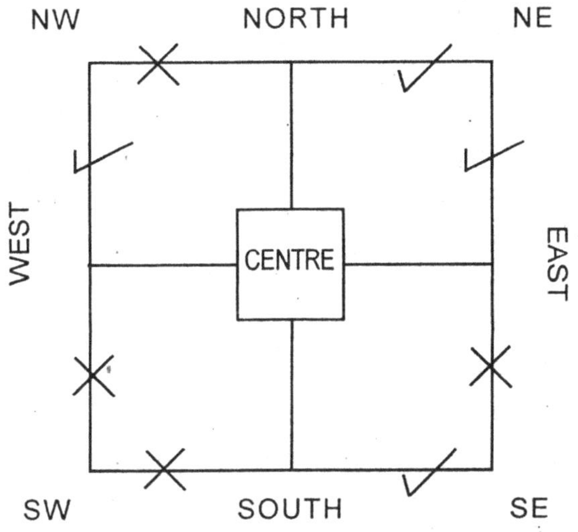

Door as per Vaastu

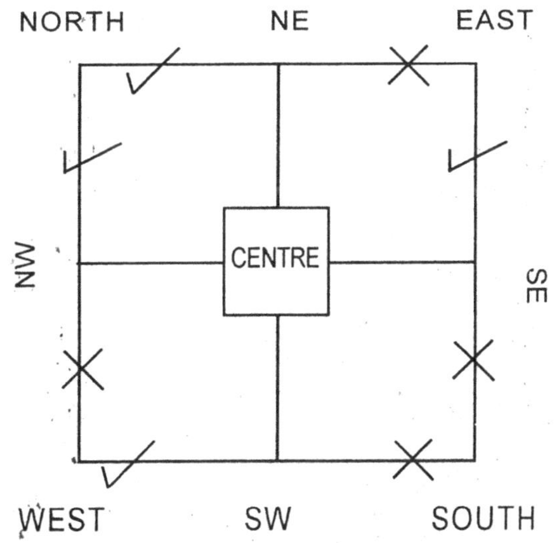

Door as per Vaastu in a *Vidisha* Plot

- If there is an obstruction in front of the main entrance such as electricity pole, column, open drain or edged corner of the building opposite the house, it is called door penetration. This is an inauspicious condition. It creates hurdles in love and marriage. This defect is not applicable if these obstructions are at a distance double the height of the house. This defect is removed if there is a public road in between. This is also not applicable when it is present in left, right or back of the house.

- When a public road stops in front of the house or enters straight from the front, it is called *'Vithishula'* (road assault). Some of these are auspicious and some are inauspicious.
- Couples living in an auspicious *'Vithishula'*, spend happy married life.

Auspicious *Vithishula*

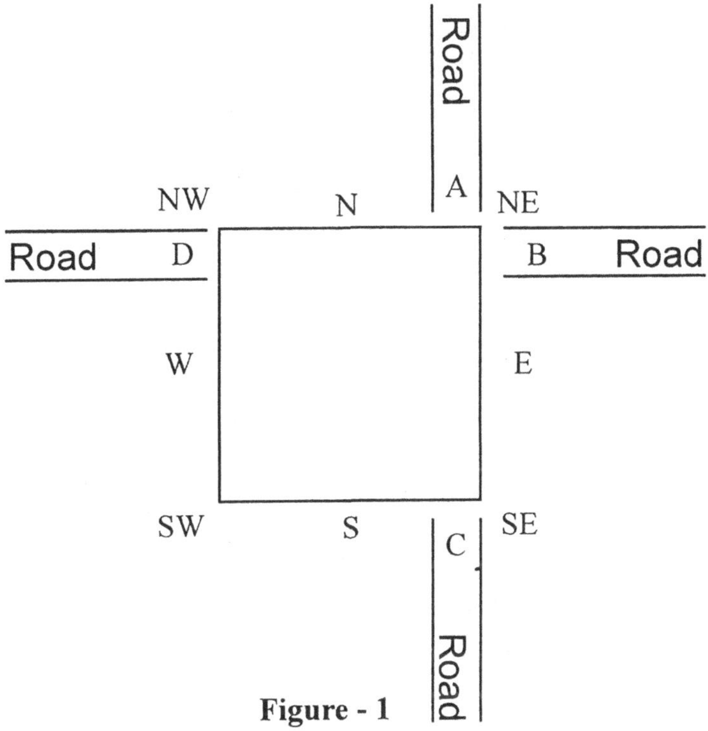

Figure - 1

Four *Vithishulas* have been depicted in the figure:

A- Entrance of the *Vithishula* from the north of the northeast zone.

B- Entrance of the *Vithishula* from east of the northeast zone.

C- Entrance of the *Vithishula* from the south of the southeast zone.

D- Entrance of the *Vithishula* from the west of the northwest zone.

- Couples living in the house on a plot with inauspicious *Vithishula* spend miserable life. They face a lot of troubles in life.

Inauspicious *Vithishula*

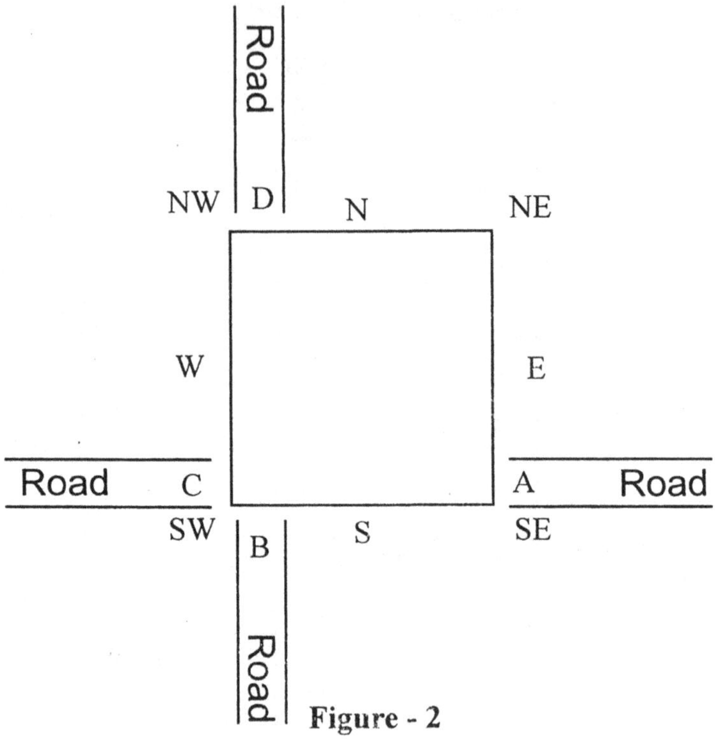

Figure - 2

Four inauspicious *Vithishula* have been depicted in the figure:

A- Entrance of the *Vithishula* from east of the southeast zone.

B- Entrance of the *Vithishula* from south of the southwest zone.

C- Entrance of the *Vithishula* from west of the southwest zone.

D- Entrance of the *Vithishula* from north of the northwest zone.

- Plots of the houses, which are situated on a square (place where four roads meet), are generally cut or rounded. If the southeast zone, southwest zone or northwest zone of the plot is cut, then there is no problem. But if the northeast zone of the plot is cut then it is inauspicious.

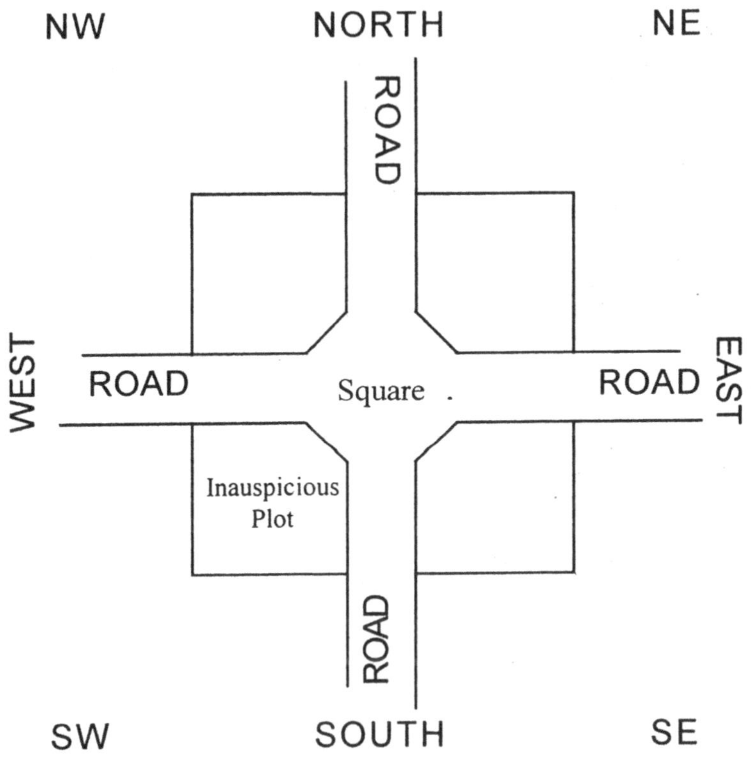

Three auspicious and one inauspicious plot on a square

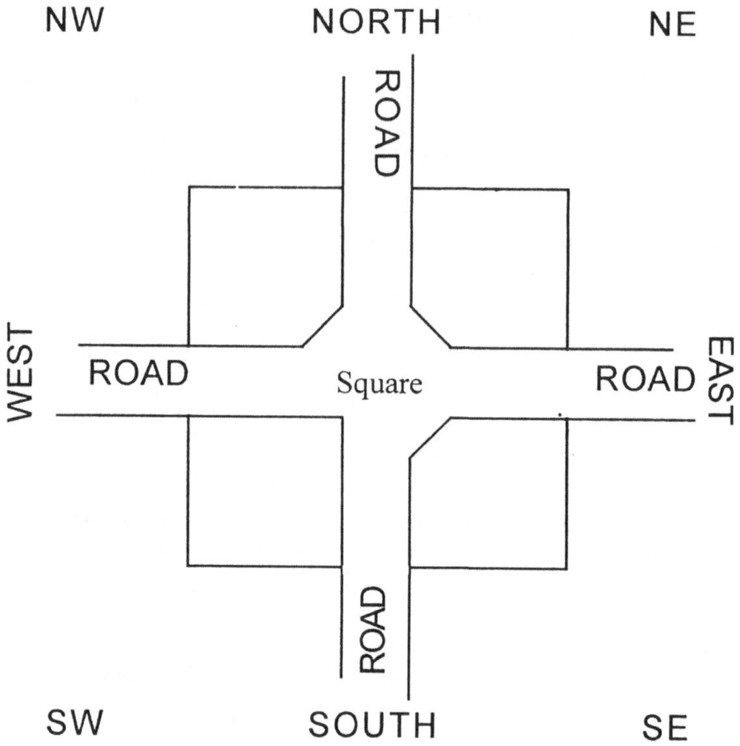

All four auspicious plots on a square

Most of the plots in the colonies developed by the developing authorities or city development trusts, have adjoining main entrances. Out of these on only one plot a house as per the Vaastu can be constructed. Couples living in such houses are happy, whereas, on the other plot a house as per Vaastu can not be constructed. Sometimes both plots are not as per Vaastu. Hence the couples living there are happy. Therefore, never construct house on a plot opposite to Vaastu.

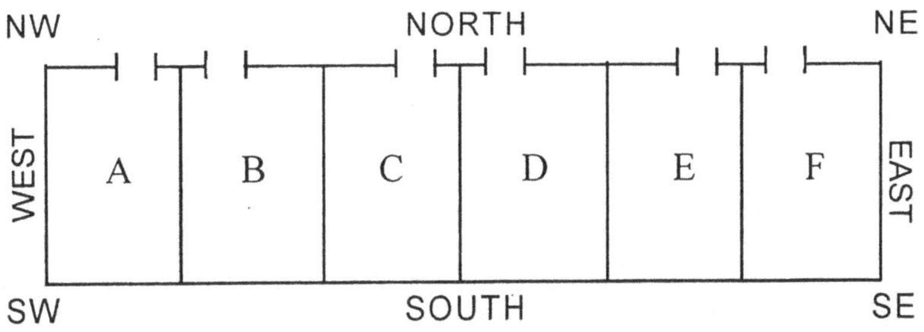

A, C & E plots are as per Vaastu & B,D & are not

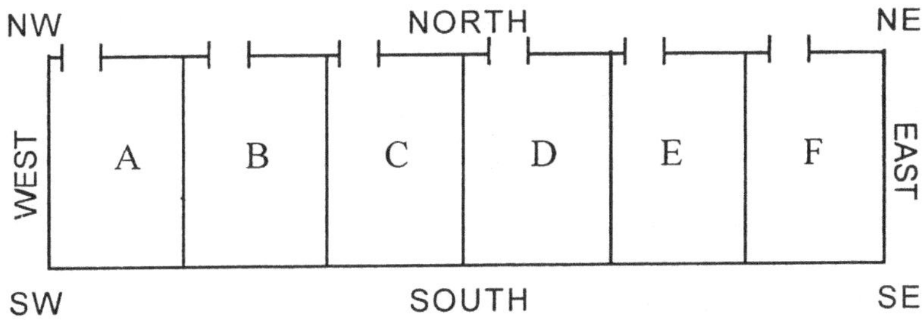

All the plots in this line are not as per Vaastu

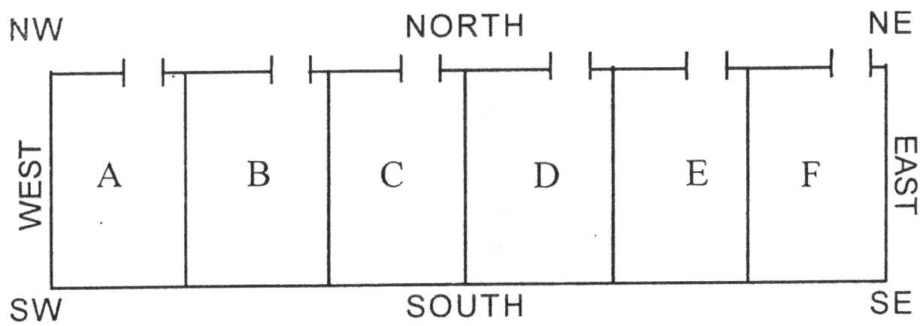

All the plots in this line are as per Vaastu

Any building should not be on a "T" junction, no matter whether it is a residence or an office. It is a very inauspicious road penetration, which creates miserable incidences in the married lives of the residents.

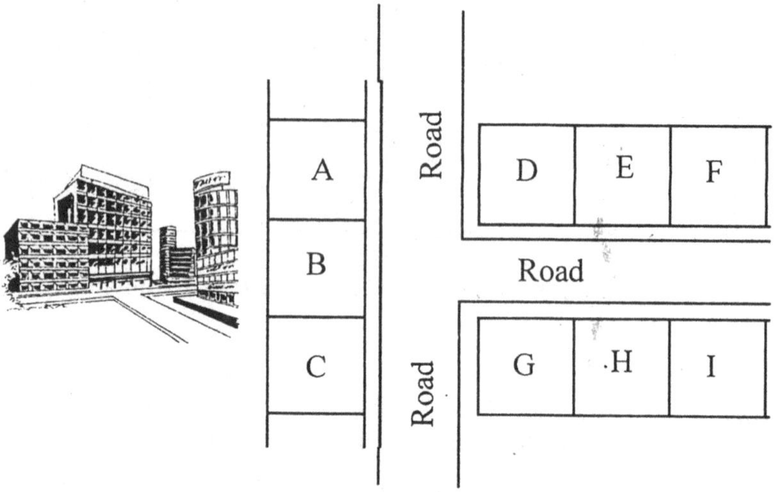

Plot B on a "T" junction

When your house is very lower or higher than the buildings in its surrounding, it is very inauspicious. People living in such houses face difficulty in their marriages.

One unsafe tall building among tiny buildings

- Do not even think about living in a place which has a tall building or any other construction in front of it. If there is a big building behind your building, it is auspicious.
- Never live in a house on either side of the dead end road. Children in such houses face problems in their marriage because the energy of such houses has no exit.

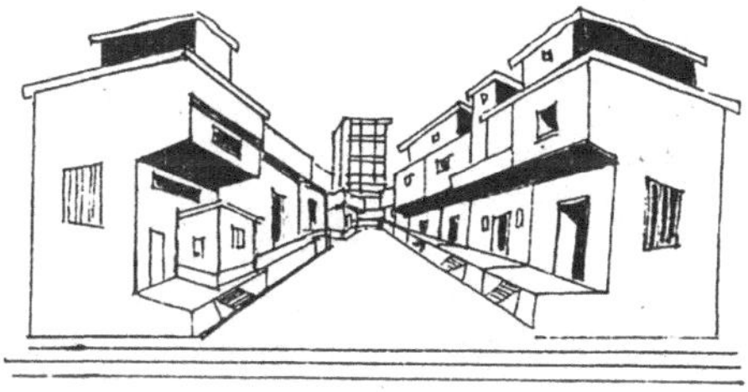

A	B	C	D	E	F
		Road			
G	H	I	J	K	L

Plots A&G on the dead end are inauspicious

- Basements are made in many houses. It has been observed that 90% of them are not constructed as per Vaastu and give inauspicious results. A lot of care has to be taken if the basement is to be constructed as per Vaastu. Hence a learned Vaastu specialist should be consulted prior to the construction or use of a basement. People using basement that are not as per Vaastu suffer tremendous physical, mental and financial troubles. It affects the married life too.

- Do not sit or lie below any hanging beam or loft in the house. It creates mental tension, which in turn affects the love and affection. Even if , due to some compulsion if it is necessary to sit or lie down below any hanging beam or loft then this defect should be removed. This can be done by putting two flutes, tied either red with ribbons, on either side of the beam or loft. This is a remedy of Feng Shui.

- An underground water tank, well, bore-well or septic tank in the northwest zone of the house is inauspicious. Even if it is lower due to any reason then also it is inauspicious. The girl of such families remains out most of the time and many times do marriage on their own without informing anybody.

- The bedroom of a marriageable girl should be in the northwest zone. This creates the possibility of marriage soon. The bed should be along with the wall in the west side, which could be used from three sides.

- Bedroom of marriageable sons should be in the northeast zone, west or south direction. They should sleep keeping their legs in the north and head in the south.

- If there is some place below the bed then put some off season clothing in it only. Do not make your bed a junkyard. If the junk is kept below the bed it creates mental unrest for the person sleeping in the same. This in turn creates quarrels on very insignificant things and disturbs the marriage.

- Marriageable children should always sleep in a double bed. No matter if they sleep in it alone. This increases the possibility of finding their life partner. There should not be any beam or loft above the bed. It is inauspicious.

- Do not sleep in the bed with two separate mattresses. There must be only single mattress of the size of the double bed. This increases the possibility of the meeting of two people.

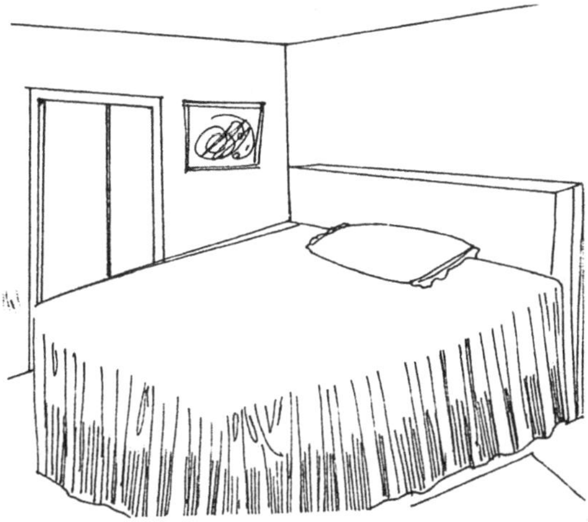

- The bed should be useable from both sides. It should never be kept along side of a wall. This decreases the possibility of finding a life partner.
- You should sit facing east or north direction while some body visits your house for your marriage. Thus you will influence the person sitting opposite to you.

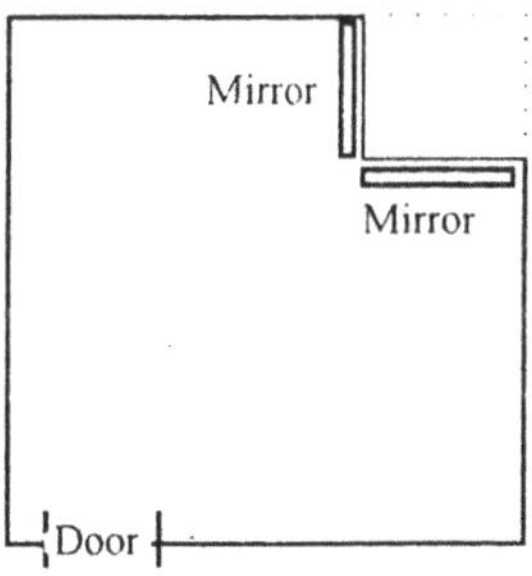

Love corner is cut as per Feng Shui

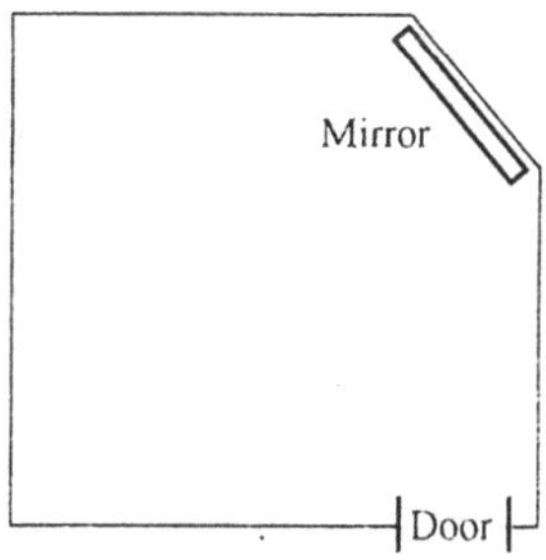

- You cannot find your love if the love corner is cut as per Feng Shui. In such cases a mirror of medium size should be put in the love zone of the room in such a way that it shows full face of the person. The mirror should be free of any dirt or spot. You can find your love due to increase in the positive energy by this treatment.

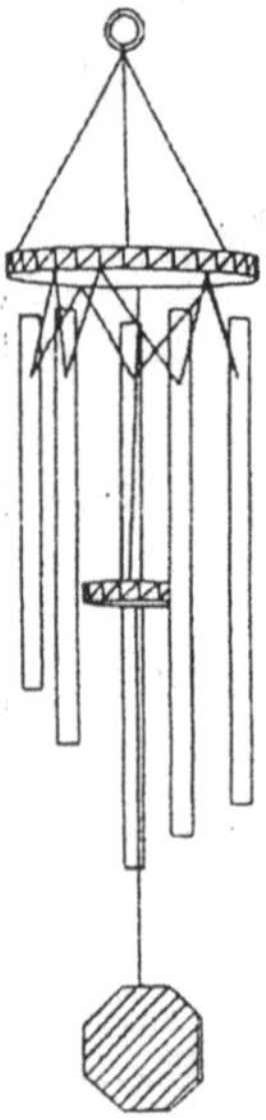

- To get favourable results the wind chimes are used in Feng Shui. If the wind chimes are placed in the right hand side corner of the wall opposite to the main entrance of the room of unmarried children of the family, it excites the love corner. Love corner is filled with positive energy by the vibrations produced by the sweet sound. Metal bell is not that effective due to its loud sound.

- Light pink colour for the curtains in the rooms of marriageable children is auspicious as per Feng Shui.

- It is auspicious to put male-female 'Lovebirds' and painting, photo or idol of the 'Mandarin Duck', which are signs of romance, in the right-hand side corner of the wall opposite to the main entrance of the bedroom. This increases the chances of the marriage of the unmarried persons.

- Do not put photographs, paintings or idol of the violent beasts and birds, with sorrow feelings, crying, sunset, drowning ship or stagnant water in the rooms of the marriageable children. These bring disappointment and frustration in life.
- Peonia flower is related to the ladies in China as per Feng Shui. It is auspicious to put them or their photograph in the corner of the wall opposite to the main entrance of the bedroom of the unmarried girl.

- Do not keep green plants in the bedroom of the marriageable children. These increase the negative "Yin" energy, which obstructs the marriage.

- The right-hand side corner of the wall opposite to the door of the drawing room of the house is filled with more energy if a crystal ball is kept there, as per Feng Shui. Your relations with your family, relatives and friends are happy, which makes your married life happy.

Double Happiness Symbol

- The red coloured "Double Happiness Symbol", as per Feng Shui is very effective. That region is filled with energy wherever it is placed. It should be placed in the marriage region of the bedroom in the right-hand side corner on the wall opposite to the main entrance. It makes the married life happy.

- If business related stuff like files and computer etc. are kept in the bedroom of the marriageable children, it may delay the chances of marriage.

- Keep a knife beneath your pillow, if you have bad thought or dreams about your love relations. This will remove bad thoughts from your mind.

- Do not put the photograph of the drowning ship like the "Titanic". Such photographs take your life downwards.
- Placing some gold fishes in a fish pot in the house increases fortune. It is auspicious, if out of these eight are red or golden in colour and one is black. The drawing room of the house is the best place to keep the fish pot. It should be placed in the right-hand side of the door of the drawing room.

- Water is wealth as per Vaastu and Feng Shui, both. A leaking tap is inauspicious in the kitchen or in anyplace of the house. It should be fixed at once.

- It is inauspicious to have opening of the door of toilets on either side of the main entrance of the house. This spreads negative energy in the house. In such a condition the door of the toilet should be closed and constructed in other side.

- Upward or downward staircases opposite to the main entrance of the house are inauspicious, as per Feng Shui. This defect could be removed by placing wind chimes of five rods outside of the main entrance.

- End of an upward staircase opposite to the main entrance of the house is inauspicious, as per Feng Shui. This defect could be removed by placing the concave mirror, Pa-Kua on the frame of the main entrance.

- Beginning of an upward staircase opposite to the main entrance of the house is inauspicious, as per Feng Shui. In such a condition the floor of the frame of the door of main entrance should be made 2 inches high.

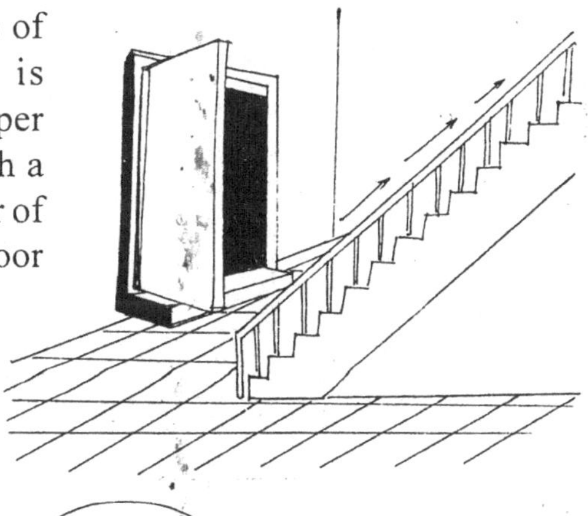

- Keeping fresh flowers in the house increases happiness. The flowers should be removed as soon as they become dry as the stale and withered flowers produce negative energy. You can keep artificial plants if you do not have green plants. These require minimum care. They look fresh with cleaning any time.
- For happy married life cactus, dry flowers, heads of the beasts and skin etc. should be removed form the house. They produce negative energy.

- Bonsai plants may look beautiful but are symbols of obstruction in the married life. They should not be kept in the house.

- Mirror is very significant in Feng Shui. Octagonal shape is supposed to be auspicious in China. There is a small mirror in the centre of octagonal mirror, Pa-Kua. This becomes very powerful by centering the energy. Pa-Kua mirror returns back the inauspicious energy (poisonous arrows), when put either inside or outside of the main entrance or window.

- Beautiful earthen flowerpots should be kept on either side of the main entrance of the house. These help in the increase of happiness in the married life by enhancing the positive energy entering the house. These plants should not be of pointed and thorny leaves. They should be of broad leaves.

- Auspicious symbols such as *Swastika*, *Om*, Trident and Cross etc. should be put as per faith. A horseshoe can also be put on the entrance of the house for increase in the fortune.

- Small bells or bouquet of flowers should be placed outside the main entrance of the house. This invites the fortune in the house.

- A call bell should be placed on the main gate of the house. Informing the arrival by knocking or calling destroys the positive energy gathered in the main entrance of the house. Hence the call bell should always be kept in the working condition.

- To give entrance to the maximum positive energy in the house the main door should be opened clockwise without making any noise.

- Automatic opening and closing of the main door of the house is inauspicious. The door should not be too big or too small in comparison to the size of the room. The hinges of the door should be oiled, if the door squeaks, while opening and closing. The noise produced by the hinges of a rusted door irritates.
- It is inauspicious to have another door adjacent to the main door of the house, as per Feng Shui. It will create problems in finding proper match for life partner.
- There should not be any door inside the house bigger than the main door. The inner door of the house should be of two panes and open inside. This facilitates the entrance of the positive energy in the house.
- It is defective to have windows on both the sides of the main door of the house. It is believed that the fortune flows out through them. Plants with round leaves should be hanged in earthen pots on windows, in such a condition.

- Do not plant climbers in the garden near main entrance of the house. They produce many problems in your life.
- Placing any type of mirror on the main door of the house is not advisable as it reflects out the auspicious energy entering the house. Due to this many good opportunities of finding a good life partner are lost.

- Do not obstruct the way by keeping your cycle, scooter or car etc. in front of the main door of the house. These create hurdles in the way of good opportunities in your life.

- Positive energy entering the house is obstructed when footwears are put in front of the main entrance.

- For the entry of the positive energy in the house without any problem, the main entrance and its surroundings should be kept clean.

- The decoration of the main door of the house, such as colour and polish, should be kept up-to-date to invite positive energy in the house. A broken, bad, dirty and rusted main door produces negative energy.

• Vibrations produced by the ringing of a small temple bell in the house, in morning and evening, destroy the negative energy of the house.

• It is auspicious to keep dry sea salt in a glass bowl, in all the toilets of the house, which absorbs the negative energy of the surroundings. This salt should be replaced when wet due to moisture.

• Negative energy of the house is destroyed and positive energy is increased when the floor is wiped with salt water.

- Any non-working television set, radio, tape recorder or clock should not be kept in the house. These things create troubles in life, which affect the married life.

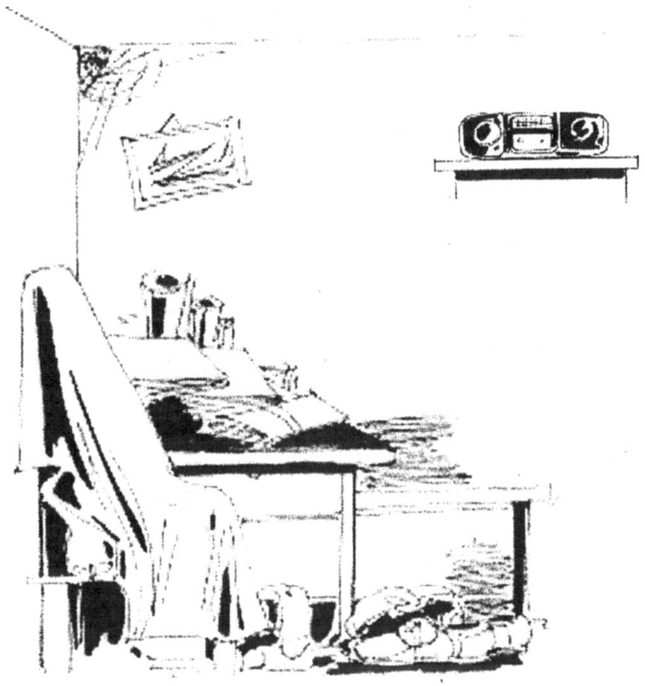

- Negative energy of the house is increased by unused stuff, disordered files and furniture and spider's webs. This is fatal for your married life.
- The house should not be situated near a big hospital, cremation ground, butchery and police station. The gloomy atmosphere of such places produces negative energy, which affects the mental status of the marriageable children badly.
- Do not purchase the house of unsuccessful and unfortunate persons, because there must be some sort of Vaastu defect, which will also make your married life miserable. Such a house can only be used after the removal of Vaastu defects.

IDEAL BEDROOM OF MARRIED COUPLE

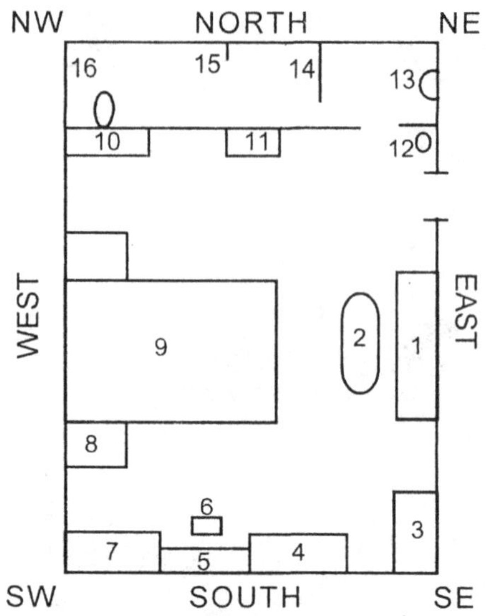

1.	Sofa	2.	Coffee Table
3.	TV/Computer	4.	Safe for Wife
5.	Dressing Table	6.	Stool
7.	Safe for Husband	8.	Bedside Table
9.	Bed	10.	Showcase/ Safe
11.	Cooler/ Fridge	12.	Drinking Water
13.	Washbasin	14.	Curtain/ Door
15.	Shower	16.	Commode

VAASTU AND DECORATION OF MARRIAGE VENUE

I attended the marriage of the daughter of a rich person, a few days back in Indore. This being the first marriage in the family the arrangement was grand. The marriage garden was beautifully decorated. A famouse caterer of the city did the catering. In a nutshell we can say that everything was done lavishly. In spite of all these grand arrangements, there was a small dispute among the relatives of the groom and bridegroom on some very insignificant thing. Guests did not like the food although it was costly, and there was chaos in the party. All the guests and the family members of the groom and bridegroom were disappointed in the end.

A Bhopal based rich Sikh family, having high social status, enthusiastically arranged a grand cocktail party on the occasion of the first *"Lohiri"* of their first son. Here also the mood of the party was spoiled by a quarrel among the guests, which turned into a sort of manhandling.

Similarly, Mr. Ramesh, who hails from a middle class family, organized a party on the occasion of the marriage of his son, in a public garden. It was a systematically arranged low budget function. Everybody enjoyed the food and praised the arrangements.

Mr. Chopra of Indore consulted me for the reception of the marriage of their daughter. I suggested some small but essential changes in the tent, lighting and stage arrangement to them. The whole function was a success. All the guests and relatives were happy and praised the arrangements. The whole function was good and more successful than expected by the Chopra family. This added to the fame of them.

I have attended many functions, somewhere people would enjoy and appreciate the arrangements and somewhere they would crticize the same. It is the case in most of the marriages also.

I have analysed above-mentioned functions on the basis of Vaastu principles, as a Vaastu consultant. The arrangements of the functions of Indore and Bhopal were not as per Vaastu and due this these functions were flop shows, whereas the function of Shri Ramesh Bhai of Ujjain was a great success due to all arrangements made as per Vaastu.

These days the functions of engagements and marriage are grand. To make these occasions memorable for a long time people spend lavishly to make the arrangements attractive and unique. Sometimes when the arrangements and decoration of a function are not as per Vaastu, it is unsuccessful and the organizer gets bad name instead of prestige. These functions could be helpful in increasing the name and fame of the organizer, if some basic principles of Vaastu and Feng Shui are followed as given below while making the arrangements.

- The place of the function should be such that the tent could be in square or rectangle shape.
- To make the presence of all the invitees sure, the main

entrance of the place should be as shown in the figure.

- There should not be any penetration, electricity pole or tree etc. in front of the entrance.
- The sitting arrangement of the groom and bridegroom on the stage should be somewhere from south of the centre to west of the centre. They should sit facing east or north.
- The stage for the orchestra can be kept on either side the place for the groom and bridegroom.
- The staircase for going up and coming down from the stage should be as per the figure. These should be perfectly as directed by the sign in figure.
- The sitting arrangement for the guest opposite the stage should be as per Feng Shui, so as to allow them a look of the entrants.
- The marriage altar (sacred fire) should be kept in the southeast zone. The generator should also be kept in the same zone.
- It is better to follow the colour principles of Feng Shui to the maximum extent, while doing the light decoration of the tent. For example, there should be blue colour in the tent towards main entrance, red opposite to it, white or light pink to the right and green to the left.
- The arrangement for water should be in the northeast zone.
- The kitchen and *tandoor* should be in the southeast zone.
- The arrangements for water and fire, i.e. *tandoor* and drinking water should not be near each other.
- The stalls of the food should be kept clockwise.
- The stake of the plates and salad should not be kept in the centre of the function.
- The water will wash away the fame if water tank is kept in the region of fame. The centre of the wall opposite to the main entrance is the region of fame.
- The place of the function will look open and airy, even if it is small, if the arrangements of the tent, stage and gate are done as per Vaastu.

- The function will be very systematic and people will praise if all the arrangements are done as per the Vaastu and Feng Shui principles, no matter whether it is big or small. You will gain prestige. It will be worth spending. The function will be graceful. This will give you a happy feeling forever and be an unforgettable function for you and your guests.

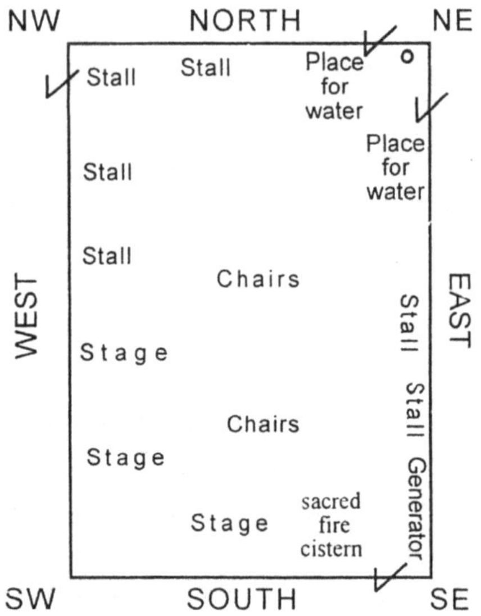

Map of the marriage tent as per Vaastu

MARRIAGE PREMISES AND VAASTU

Nowadays marriage premises, banquet halls or marriage gardens are taken on rent for the marriage and other small family functions due to growing population and shrinking place in the houses. Marriage premises equipped with all the amenities are being constructed from small towns to the metros of the country due to their increasing use. It has been observed that some of these are always booked for some or other function while some are booked seldom in spite of being equipped with all the amenities.

With a view for investment and to earn money, Mr. Shah a successful businessman, constructed a marriage premises in a very good locality of Ahmedabad. He constructed a beautiful marriage garden, fully equipped with all the modern amenities, on a very costly plot. Unfortunately, the plot itself was not as per Vaastu. He completed the construction overlooking this fact. After investing heavily on this project Mr. Shah is not earning anything out of this and has to spend something on and off till date, because of the running expenses, such as water and electricity.

The north of the northeast zone of the marriage premises of Mr. Shah was depressed, which is a significant Vaastu defect. The entrance of the premises is in the north of the northwest zone. The stage for the bride and bridegroom is three feet high in the north of the northeast zone.

I have suggested Mr. Shah to make the plot as per Vaastu, either by increasing the north of the northeast zone making it right-angled or decrease the north and northwest zone to make them right-angled. This will make the northeast zone of 90^0 and make the plot as per Vaastu. The stage for the bride and bridegroom should be in the south or west direction instead of north of the northwest zone.

The marriage premises are airy, open and the functions held are graceful if the following Vaastu principles are followed at the time of construction. The guests praise the family arranging the function and the owner of the premises gets attractive returns on his investment.

- The plot for the marriage premises should be right-angled and in the centre or easily accessible place of the city.
- The level of the plot should be either uniform or higher in the east, north and northeast zone and lower in the west, south and southwest zone.
- The underground water source for the premises should be in the east, north or northeast zone. There are many troubles if the underground water source is kept in any other direction. Overhead water tank of the premises should be in the south or west.
- The lawn of the premises should be in the east, north or northeast zone. This place is suitable for the functions too. Hence ample open space should be left in the east and north of the plot. A small temple can also be constructed in this region, if required.
- The construction of the building in the marriage premises should be done in the southwest zone and the rooms therein should be right-angled. They should never be odd shaped. Toilet and bathroom can also be constructed with these rooms, but these should never be constructed in the northeast zone of the room.
- Maximum windows of the building of the marriage premises should be in the east or north. They should be minimum in the west and south direction.
- The staircase should be in the west, south or southwest zone with a right-hand turn while ascending, in the building of the premises.
- The guest rooms of the building in the premises should be in the west or northwest zone.
- Storeroom should be in the west or southwest zone.
- The place for the generator, motor and other electrical appliances should be in the southeast zone.
- Toilets can be constructed in the west, north or northwest

zone. Never construct toilet in the northeast zone.

- Main entrance of the marriage premises should be in the east of the northeast zone, south of the southeast zone, west of the northwest zone or north of the northeast zone. It should never be in the east of the southeast zone, south of the southwest zone, west of the southwest zone or north of the northwest zone.
- There should not be any penetration, like electricity pole and tree etc., in front of the main entrance.
- The stage for the bride-bridegroom and the orchestra should be somewhere in the centre from south to west, as per Vaastu, in such a way that they face east or north direction. The stage should never be in the east, north or northeast zone.
- The staircase for the stage should be as shown in the figure only. The ascending and descending of the guests on the stage should be clockwise.
- The ascending on the stage should be from south of the southeast zone and descending from north or east of the northeast zone, if the bride-bridegroom face east while sitting. The ascending should be from east of the northeast zone and descending from west of the northwest zone, if they face north while sitting.
- The stage for the orchestra can be constructed on either side of the stage for the bride-bridegroom in the south or west direction.
- The sitting arrangement for the guests should be as per Feng Shui so that the bride-bridegroom and guests can have a look of the entrants.
- The marriage altar (sacred fire) should be in the southeast zone. The kitchen and *tandoor* should also be in the southeast zone.
- The arrangement for the drinking water should be in the northeast zone. It inauspicious to keep fire and water together, as per Feng Shui. *Tandoor* and water arrangement should never be together.
- Eating arrangement should be in the north or west direction. The stalls for the food should be kept clockwise.

Place for the plates and *salad* should not be in the centre of the premises. The "*Brahmsthan*" in the centre of the premise and garden should always be empty.

- Parking for the guests' vehicles should be in the northwest direction.

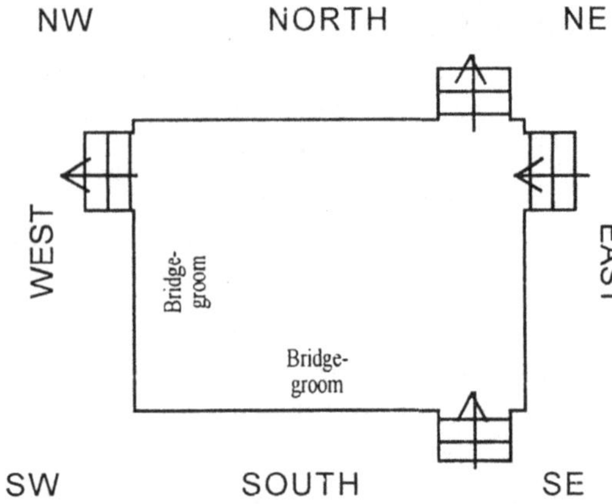

Ascending arrangement for the stage

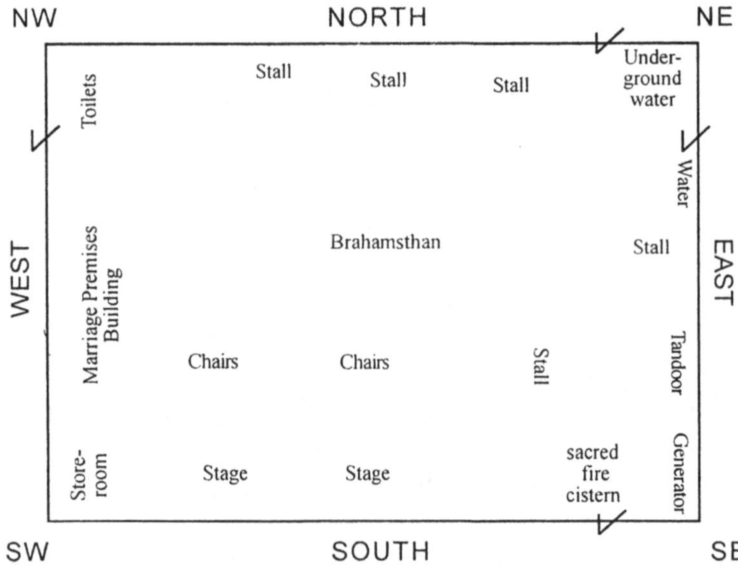

Map of the marriage premises as per Vaastu

STUDENTS – VAASTU & FENG SHUI

I find parents bothering for the career of their children in this era of competition wherever I go for Vaastu consultancy.

Recently I visited the house of Mr. Khanna of Kanpur for Vaastu consultancy. His wife was perturbed above the study of their two children. She told to me that both of them could concentrate on their studies, passed with difficulty every year and remained unwell too. I visited the study-cum-bedroom of the children. They were facing south while studying and their back was to the door. Headside of their bed was in the north direction. Thus all the conditions of study and sleeping were against the principles of Vaastu and Feng Shui.

Similarly, when I visited the house of Mr. Bhatia of Mumbai for Vaastu consultancy, his wife too was perturbed about the studies of their son. She told that their son is always in tension for his studies. He was lagging behind in his studies due to lack of concentration. I visited the study-cum-bedroom of their son too. There was a loft of 2 feet in all the directions of the room. He used to study and sleep underneath it. This caused his mental tension. This was evident from his lifestyle too.

There are many children who play and enjoy a lot and do study for a less time but pass with good marks, when their result is declared, whereas there are others who study a lot with the help of their family members but fail or pass with poor marks. Students face problems of many kinds when the study room is constructed opposite to the Vaastu and Feng Shui principles. Their career depends on good study. If the parents and children take some care and follow some simple rules of Vaastu and Feng Shui both, they will pass with good marks with less hard work and will have a bright future.

- The plot of your residence should be rectangular or square, for the bright future of your children. It should not be of irregular shape. The southwest zone of the plot should be of 90^0. Ample open space should be left in the east and north directions. Students living in such a house progress well.

- Purchase or construct your house on a place, which has deep pits, pond and river etc. to its north and east and hillocks and mound in the south and west directions. Such houses are boon for students.
- Do not purchase or construct your house where there are higher buildings, mountains, rocks or big trees like *pipal* and banyan trees in the north and east and deep pits, pond or river in the south and west directions. Such houses are the cause of failure.
- The house should be constructed in the square or rectangular shape on a right-angled plot for good fortune. Care should be taken to construct rooms with right angle. Children living in such houses do higher study.

- The house for the students should be such where the morning sun rays are approachable. To make these morning sun rays available for them in the house, the boundary wall of the house in the east and northeast zone should be lower. These are beneficial for good health of the children.
- To save the students from the harmful sun rays of noon and evening the boundary wall of the house in the west, south and southwest zone should be higher.
- It is inauspicious to have cut, depressed and round east, north and northeast zone of the house of students, because this obstructs the benefit of the morning sun rays. On the other hand, if these directions are increased then it is

auspicious. Hence, if theses directions are inauspicious, then this defect should be corrected by constructing the house right-angled.

- The students in a house with bad northeast zone will lag behind in their studies and become mentally retarded. The elder son of the house will face lot of mental and physical problems.
- Underground water tank, bore-well and well should be constructed in the east and northeast zone of the house after leaving ample open space. This water becomes very useful for drinking and bathing due to the morning sun rays. This makes the students healthy and happy.
- The east, north and northeast zone should be lower than the west, south and southwest zone of the house. The lower northeast zone invites bad luck and the students there face many problems.
- The main entrance of the house should be in the left-hand side in an east or south facing house. It should in the right-hand side if the house is west or south facing. Thus the entrance to the house should be as shown in the figure. Students face many problems if the entrance is kept where it is crossed in the figure.

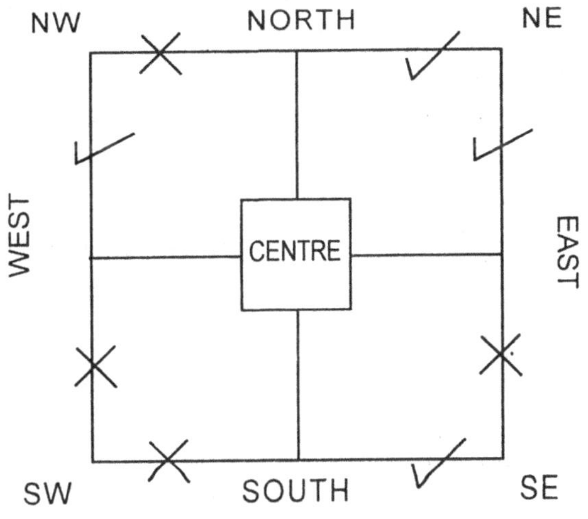

Place for main entrance as per Vaastu

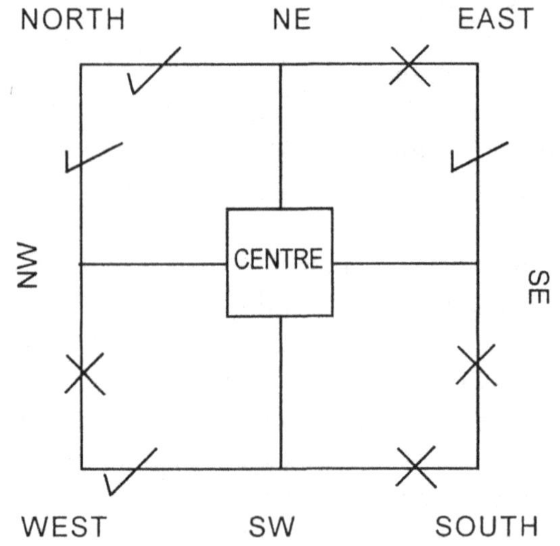

Place for main entrance as per Vaastu in a *Vidisha* plot

- If there is an obstruction, such as electricity pole, column, tree, open drain or edged corner of any other building etc., opposite to the main entrance of the house, it is called penetration. Any penetration is inauspicious, as it create problems in the career of students. But if the penetration is at a distance double the height of the house then it is ineffective. If there is a public road in between the house and penetration then also this defect is null. If such a penetration is present in the back or either side of the house then also it is ineffective.
- Money is flushed out and you get bad name if the toilet is in the northeast zone of the house. These days it is a fashion to decorate the toilets and bathrooms. It is against Vaastu because due to this the positive energy of the house is flushed out.
- No building, whether office or home, should be on a "T" junction. This is a very inauspicious road penetration, which creates miserable incidences in the lives of the students.

- Do not even think of studying in a building, in front of which there is very high building or some other construction work is going on. If there is a big building behind your building, it auspicious.
- If your house is out of proportion to the surrounding (either too high or too small) then it is inauspicious. The students studying in such houses lag behind in the studies.
- Do not live in a house on any side of the dead end of a road. The students do not get desired success in such houses because the there is no exit for the energy in them.
- Basements are constructed in many houses. It has been observed that most of them are constructed against Vaastu and give inauspicious results. Lot of care has to be taken to construct the basement as per Vaastu. One should consult an experienced Vaastu consultant before starting the construction of basement. Students face failure because of the tremendous problems caused by basements constructed against Vaastu.

- Sleeping below a loft or beam should be avoided as it creates mental tension. Two flutes should be tied in a red ribbon at 45 to remove this defect as per Feng Shui, if due to compulsion it is required to sleep or study beneath the beam or loft.

- Students should face east or north while studying. This will help them to understand the subject easily.

- There is a possibility of betrayal, if students study keeping their back to the door of the room.
- The study room should always be constructed in the west or northeast zone of the building. It should never be in the southwest or southeast zone.

- To take the full advantage of the morning sun rays entering the room, the windows and door should be kept open in the morning hours, but to avoid the harmful noon and evening sun rays these should be kept closed at the evening time.
- The window in the study room, if present, should always be in the east, west or north direction to get the advantage of the positive energy of the sun. The windows should be kept closed, if the same are in the south direction to save from the negative energy.

- The computer, if being used should be placed anywhere in between southeast zone to south and west. Do not place the computer in the northeast zone. Computer placed in the northeast zone is sparingly used.
- A photograph or idol of the God can be placed, for the mental peace, in the northeast zone. Drinking water can also be placed here.

- The room can be converted into a study-cum-bedroom if students sleep in it.
- Students should always sleep keeping their head in the south or west direction. Sleeping with head in the south keeps good health and head in the west keeps the longing for study on.
- Keep the door of the toilet always closed, if one is attached to the study room. Do not decorate the toilet much. Take care of the cleaning of the toilet.
- The bookracks can be placed in the south and west directions. Do not keep them in the southwest or northwest zone. Students sparingly read books kept in the racks in southwest zone and there is threat of theft of the books in the racks of northwest zone.
- Do not keep the books in an open rack. Put a door over the rack as books kept in the open produce negative energy, which disturbs health.
- There should not be any type of junk like unused old books and cloths in the room. If you want to make a good career.

- A feeling of cooperation will be developed among the children studying in one room, if group photograph of them in jovial mood is placed there.

- As per Feng Shui hanging a crystal ball on the left corner of the wall of the entrance of the study room and keeping globe on the study table give excellent success. This increases the region of education and wisdom as per Feng Shui.

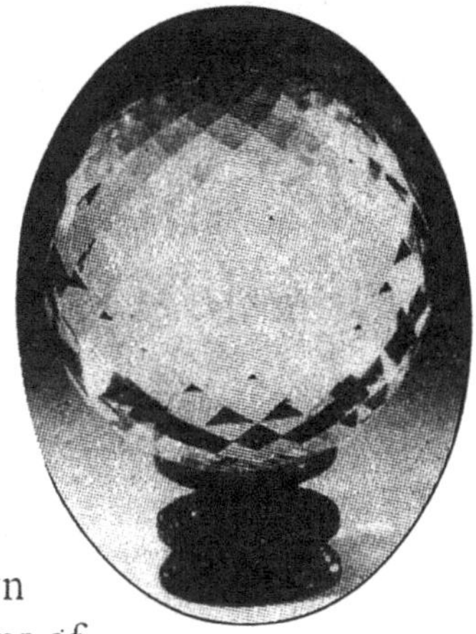

- It is better to have light blue, light green and light brown colour on the walls and curtains of the study room. White colour makes them lazy.
- Remove cactus, dry flowers, head of beasts and skin etc. from the study room, to get good results, because these produce negative energy.
- Bonsai plants may look beautiful but are symbols of obstruction in the intellectual development. Hence they should not be kept in the study room.

- Put a bulb of high power on the door of the study room and keep it on round the clock if the students do not get desired results.

IDEAL STUDY CUM BEDROOM FOR STUDENTS

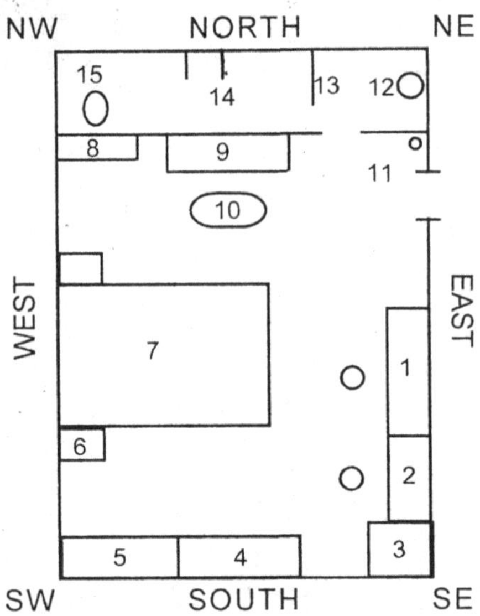

1. Study Table
2. Computer
3. Television
4. Book Racks
5. Safe
6. Bedside Table
7. Bed
8. Dressing Table
9. Sofa
10. Tea Table
11. Drinking Water
12. Washbasin
13. Curtain
14. Tap
15. Commode

EFFECTIVE MANTRA FOR SUCCESS IN STUDY

Om sumukhashchekdantashch kapilo gajkarnakah!
Lambodarashch vikato vighnanasho vinayakah!!
Dhumraketurganadhyaksho bhalchandro gajananah!
dwadshaitani namani yah pathekshanuyadapi!!
vidhyarambhe vivahe ch praveshe nirgame tatha!
sangrame sankate chaiv vighnastasya na jayate!!

Students never fail if above Mantra is chanted 24 times a day

विद्या अध्ययन में सफलता पाने का प्रभावशाली मंत्र

ऊँ सुमुखश्चैकदन्तश्च कपिलो गजकर्णकः।
लंबोदरश्च विकटो विघ्ननाशो विनायकः।।
धूम्रकेतुर्गणाध्यक्षो भालचन्द्रो गजाननः।
द्वादशैतानि नामानि यः पठेक्ष्छणुयादपि।।
विद्यारम्भे विवाहे च प्रवेशे निर्गमे तथा।
संग्रामे संकटे चैव विघ्नस्तस्य न जायते।।

उपरोक्त मंत्र का प्रतिदिन 24 बार जाप करने से विद्यार्थी परीक्षा में असफल नहीं होते हैं।

SCHOOL AND VAASTU

Everbody accepts the importance of education in this 21st century. Well-planned study and training are essential to get success in this era of high technique and competition. One has to go to various educational institutes for good and higher education. Financial budgets of families are disturbed by the costly fees structure of these institutes sometimes. It is sad to note that most of these institutes do not fulfil the aim of the students even after charging exorbitant fees.

The students of an educational institute will get happy atmosphere if it is constructed and decorated as per Vaastu as given below. Their mental concentration will increase. This will produce positive results and their aim will be fulfilled. The fame of the institute will be increased and the students will progress. The atmosphere of the institute will be full of love and friendly feelings, which are required much today.

- The building of the school should be on a right-angled plot.
- Underground water source such as tank, well or bore-well should be in east, north or northeast zone.
- Open space for playground should be in the east direction.
- The main entrance of the school should be in the east or north direction. It is as per Vaastu and auspicious too.
- The building of school can be constructed in the west or south direction. The building should be constructed in the west or south of the southwest zone, if it is to be constructed in "L" shape. This will leave open space in the east and north directions.
- The staircase of the building can be constructed anywhere in the southwest zone. It should never be constructed in the northeast zone.

- Toilet and bathroom can be constructed in the west of the northwest zone. They should never be in the northeast zone.
- Overhead water tank should be in the northwest zone.
- No basement should be constructed in the school building.
- The length to width ratio of the classrooms should not be more than 1:2. all the rooms should be right-angled.
- Black board of the class should be in the west direction. A small dais can be constructed here for the teachers.
- There should not be any beam any where in the classroom. This will create tension in the students sitting beneath it.
- The entrance to the classroom should be in the north or east of the northeast zone. The door should always be of two panes and opening inside.
- The colour of the classroom and its curtains should be light blue, light green or light brown. White colour makes the students lazy. Rest of the school building can be coloured in light cream or white. Dark colours bring violence in the behavior of the students.
- The position of the door of the class should be such that the students and teachers should not have their back towards it, while studying.
- There must be photographs of the great men in the classrooms to inspire the students.
- The laboratory and computer room should be in the west with doors opening in the east direction.
- Staff room and common room for the students should be in the northwest zone.
- Office of the school, where fee is deposited and admissions are given, should be in the east of the school building.
- The room of the principal of the school should be in the west, south or southwest zone with a door opening in the east direction.
- The auditorium of the school should be in the north direction with a door in the east direction.

- The stationary of the school should be kept in the west or south direction only.
- The library should be in the west of the school building.
- Arrangements for indoor games can be done in the west direction.
- There must be greenery for beautification and happy atmosphere in the school. Small plants should be in the east and north and big in the west, south and southwest zone.
- Swimming pool, if constructed, should be in the north or east direction only.
- Arrangements can be made for parking of the vehicles in the west or south directions.

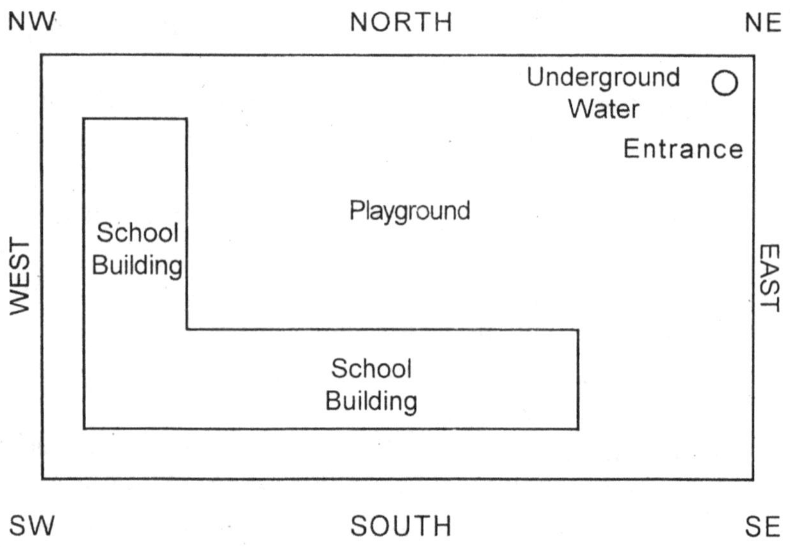

School building as per Vaastu

HOSTEL AND VAASTU

Students of today are crazy about studying in the schools and colleges of good standards. Everybody wants to take admission in good institutes. They are ready to leave their native place for this, no matter how far it is. Such students try to find a place as a paying guest, in a private hostel or the hostel of the institute where they take admission.

Parents also spend lavishly on the education of their children. They take it as an investment for an excellent career of their children. Education has become business these days. Excellent arrangements are done to attract the students by the management. The management of the education institutes with hostels provides swimming pool, recreation room and other high-class comforts to its students.

It has been observed that students are ready to take admissions in hostels of some institutes where as in some others they are not. This all depends on whether the construction of the hostel has been carried out as per Vaastu or not.

The hostel is open, airy and full of sunlight if constructed as per vaastu. The atmosphere there is beautiful and happy. Students are at ease and feel good in such a place. These hostels are always full to their capacities. Nobody likes to take admission in a hostel which is not constructed as per Vaastu and those who have taken admission want to leave as soon as possible. The atmosphere of that place is gloomy.

The directors of the hostel will make profit and the fame of the hostel will be increased if following things are taken care of at the time of construction of the hostel. The students staying: there will remain happy and get success their studies:

- The shape of the plot, where the hostel is to be constructed, should be square or rectangular. It should not be of irregular shape. The southwest zone of the plot should be with a 90^{0} angle. Ample space should be left in the east and north of the plot while carrying out the construction.
- Cut, depressed or round east, north and northeast zone of the plot are inauspicious. This creates problems for the directors of the hostel. It is auspicious to have these directions big. If this defect is present then either increasing the length or making them right angled should remove it.
- Underground water source for the hostel should be in the northeast zone. It is inauspicious if present in any other direction. Swimming pool of the hostel should be constructed in the east or north direction. Underground water source and swimming pool, if present in the centre of the hostel, create problems for students and directors both.
- Hostel should be constructed in west, south or southwest zone, if the shape is "L" or "U" to leave ample open space in the east and north directions.
- The main entrance of the hostel should be in the east of the northeast, south of the southeast, west of the northwest or north of the northeast zone. The passage to enter and exit the hostel and the doors of all the rooms of hostel should open in this direction only.
- Arrangement for the electric motor, transformer, generator and other electrical appliances of the hostel should be made in the southeast zone.
- Kitchen of the hostel should be constructed in the southeast zone, where ample air and light are available. Mixer etc. electronic appliances can be kept on a platform in the south of the kitchen. Hearth, *tandoor* and microwave

oven should be kept in the southeast zone. A storeroom can be constructed in the west or southwest zone of the kitchen.

- Arrangement for geyser should be made in the southeast zone.
- Construction of the overhead water tank can be done any where from west of the northwest zone to south of the southwest zone.
- Common and recreation rooms of the hostel should always be in the northwest zone only. Arrangement for indoor games can also be done here. Playground for the students should be in the east or north direction.
- A garden can be constructed around the hostel. Mind you, small plants should be in the east and north and big in the west and south directions of the garden.
- The reception of the hostel should be on the ground floor only. The receptionist should face east or north direction while sitting.
- The administrative office of the hostel can be in the west or south direction.
- The dining hall of the mess of the hostel should be constructed in the west of the building. The mess in charge should sit facing east or north in such a way that he should be able to look every table of the dining room.
- The rooms of the hostel should be constructed in such a way so as to provide maximum exposure of the morning sun rays to the students. The windows of the rooms should be in the east, west or north direction and never in the south direction.
- Bookshelves and safe for other stuff should be made with the wall in the west or south direction and never in the northeast zone.
- The light system of the rooms should be such that the students should not face any difficulty while studying with face in the east direction.

- Do not construct the toilet in the northeast zone, if the room has an attached toilet.
- It is better to colour the walls and curtains of the room with light blue, light green and light brown shades. The students become lazy if the colour is white.

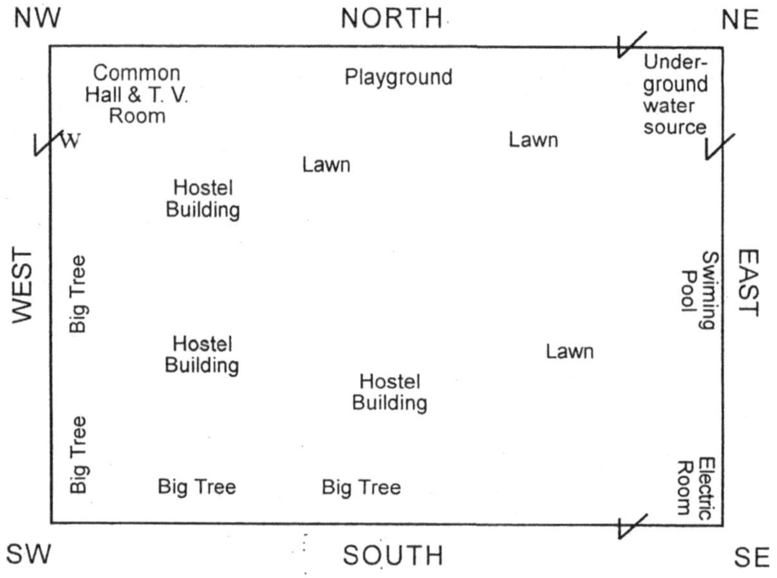

Hostel as per Vaastu

STADIUM AND VAASTU

It is very essential to play for good health. Generally, every school has a playground where the students assemble, perform drill, play and remain happy during the school hours.

The playground of every school should be prepared as per Vaastu. This will attract the students towards the playground. They will remain energetic physically and mentally. The playground of the school should be in east or north direction.

Following principles of Vaastu should be obeyed if a stadium is to be constructed in the playground of the school:

- A place with deep pits, pond and river etc. in the northeast zone and big mounds and hillocks in the southwest zone must be chosen for the stadium. Stadium in such a place gets big name and the players of there become famous.
- The plot on which the stadium is to be constructed should be of square or rectangular shape. The land should be even. The southwest corner of the land should be of 90^0. Leave ample space in the northeast zone while carrying out the construction of the stadium.
- It is inauspicious to have the north, east and northeast zone of the plot cut, depressed or round. This will create many problems for the players. On the contrary if these directions are increased then it is auspicious. If the plot shape is inauspicious then it must be corrected either by increasing or decreasing the directions.
- The north, east and northeast zone of the plot should be lower than the south, west and southwest zone. Opposite condition is unfortunate. If the northeast zone of the plot is higher then excavating the soil of this region and filling in the west and southwest zone should level it.
- A round, oval, square or octagonal stadium can be

constructed on a right-angled plot. A small stadium in east or north direction of the big stadium, can be constructed, if required.

- The underground water source of the stadium should be in the northeast zone and the overhead water tank in the west direction. The swimming pool of the stadium should only be constructed in the east or north direction.
- Arrangement for the electricity meter, lighting, public address system and other electrical appliances should be done in the southeast zone only.
- The staircase of the stadium should be in the southwest zone with a right turn while ascending.
- The higher galleries for the spectators in the stadium should be in the south, west and southwest zone. Galleries of lower height may be in any other direction. The highest gallery should be in the southwest zone and the lowest in the northeast zone.
- The main entrance and exit of the stadium should be in the east of the northeast zone, south of the southeast zone, west of the northwest zone or north of the northeast zone only.
- A storeroom in the southwest zone can be constructed to keep the sparingly used material.
- The change rooms and toilets for the players should be constructed in the northwest zone.
- The restaurant of the stadium should be in the southeast zone.
- The meditation and yoga centre of the stadium should be in the east or northeast zone of the stadium.
- The cricket pitch should be prepared in the east or north direction.
- The health club, massage room and steam bathroom should be constructed in the northwest zone. Arrangements for indoor games can also be done in this direction.
- A big score board should be constructed at a higher place in the south of the southwest zone.

- Common and recreation rooms should be constructed in the northwest zone.
- Guest room should also be constructed in the northwest zone.
- The office of the stadium should be in the north or east direction.
- The office of the secretary should be in the west or south direction and he should sit facing east direction.
- The safe of the cashier should be kept along with the south wall and open to the north direction.
- The parking place for the big vehicles can be in the west or south direction and for the smaller ones in the east or north direction.
- A garden can be made around the stadium. Mind you all the small plants should be in the east and north direction and bigger trees in the west and south direction only.

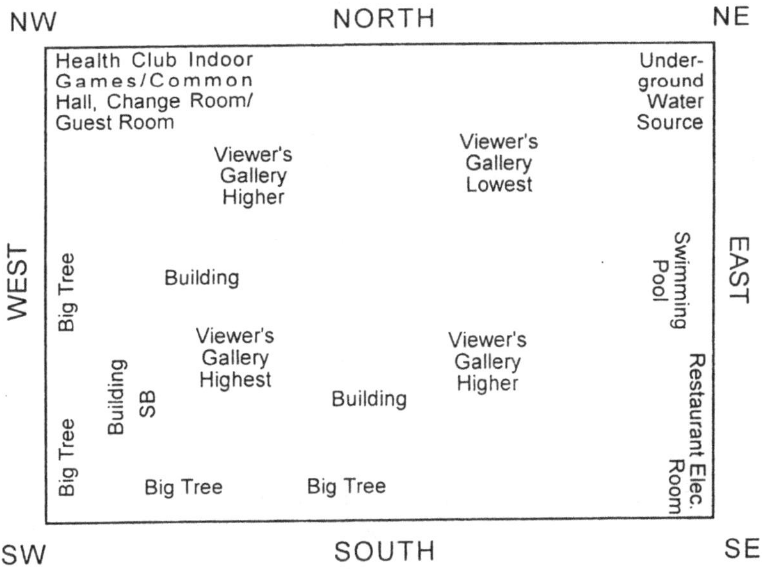

Stadium as per Vaastu

BEAUTY PARLOUR AND VAASTU

The first wish of every lady is to look beautiful and gorgeous. Many beauty parlours are working nowadays to fulfil this wish of their. Ladies wait for their turn and pay more in certain beauty parlours of a city, whereas in certain beauty parlours, which are conveniently located and equipped with all the modern facilities, rarely anybody goes. The Vaastu of a parlour plays an important role in the success of the same. A parlour constructed as per Vaastu becomes famous and earns lot. Hence the decoration of the parlour should be done as per Vaastu only.

- Beauty parlour should be made in a square or rectangular room. Do not use a room of irregular shape.
- The main entrance of the parlour should be in east of the northeast zone, south of the southeast zone, west of the northwest zone or north of the northeast zone. Never keep the main entrance in the east of the southeast zone, south, west of the southwest zone or north of the northwest zone.
- The level of the parlour should be even or lower in the north, east and northeast zone and higher in the south, west or southwest zone.
- The place of worship and drinking water should be in the northeast zone. The washbasin should be in the east or north direction.
- Mirrors should be placed on the walls of west or south directions. The sitting arrangements for the customers should also be in the same direction in such a way that they face south or west while sitting.
- Almirah should be should be provided in the south or west direction to keep the appliances and cosmetics used in the parlour.

- The massage table in the parlour should be in the west direction with an arrangement of keeping the head of the customer in the south and legs in the north direction.
- The arrangement of steam for facial treatment should be done in the southeast zone. All other electrical appliances should also be kept in the southeast zone.
- There must be any light colour like light gray or white on the walls and curtains of the parlour. Never use any dark colour.
- The cash box in the parlour should be kept such that it opens in the north direction.
- The toilet should be in the northwest zone. It should never be in the northeast zone.
- The posters of hairstyle etc. should be in the northeast zone.
- There must be separate racks for the cosmetics to be sold, in the northwest zone.
- The sofa for the waiting customers should be in the north or east direction.

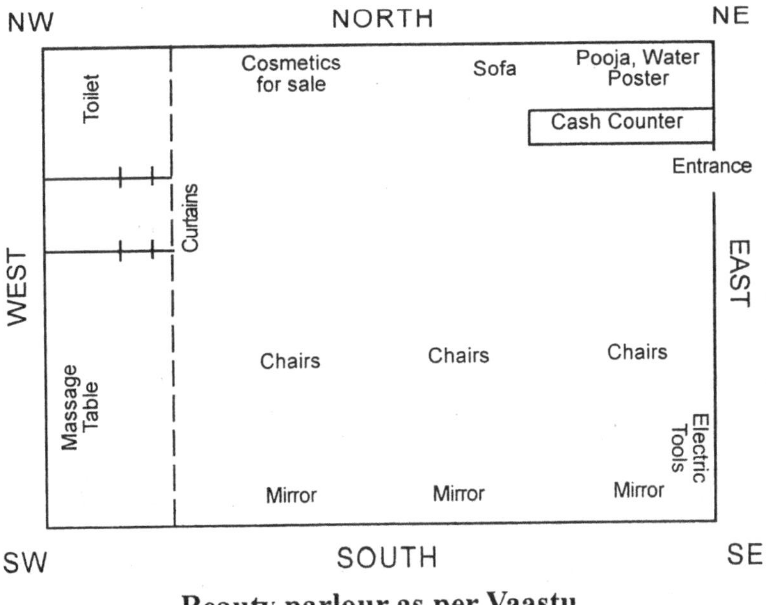

Beauty parlour as per Vaastu

BOUTIQUE AND VAASTU

Everybody wants to look different from others in the era of fashion. The craze for the designer clothes is increasing due to this. Many boutiques are working to fulfil this desire of young ladies. They get readymade clothes of their choice or get them stitched there. Some of these boutiques run successfully and earn money but others are closed due to loss. There maybe many reasons behind the success of a boutique but Vaastu plays an important role in the same.

The boutique owner earns handsomely if it is decorated as per Vaastu:

- The shop for the boutique should be in the square or rectangular shape. Never choose a shop of irregular shape.
- The main entrance of the boutique should be in the east of the northeast zone, south of the southeast zone, west of the northwest zone or north of the northeast zone. It should never be in the east of the southeast zone, south, west of the southwest zone or north of the northwest zone.
- The level of the boutique should be even or lower in the north, east and northeast zone and higher in the south, west and southwest zone.
- The place of worship and drinking water in the boutique should be in the northeast zone only.
- The mirror should be placed on the south or west wall of the boutique.
- The lower racks for the clothes in the boutique should be in the north and east direction while higher in the south and west direction.
- The clothes to be stitched should be kept in an almirah in east direction. The stuff used for stitching like thread, canvas, button and zip etc. should also be kept in the east direction only.
- Cash box of the boutique should be in such a place that the drawer of the same opens in the north direction.

- The display window of the boutique should be in the east or north direction.
- The counter to display the clothes should be in the south or west direction.
- The stitching machines, if kept in the boutique, should be in the south direction.
- The table on which the clothes are cut should be in the southwest zone.
- The table for iron should be in the southeast zone. All other electrical appliances should be kept in the same direction.
- The racks for the clothes ready for delivery should be in the north of the northwest zone.
- The colour of the walls of the boutique should be light green, light blue or bright.
- The posters and photographs of the clothes should be in the northeast zone.
- The sofa for the customers should be in the north or east direction.

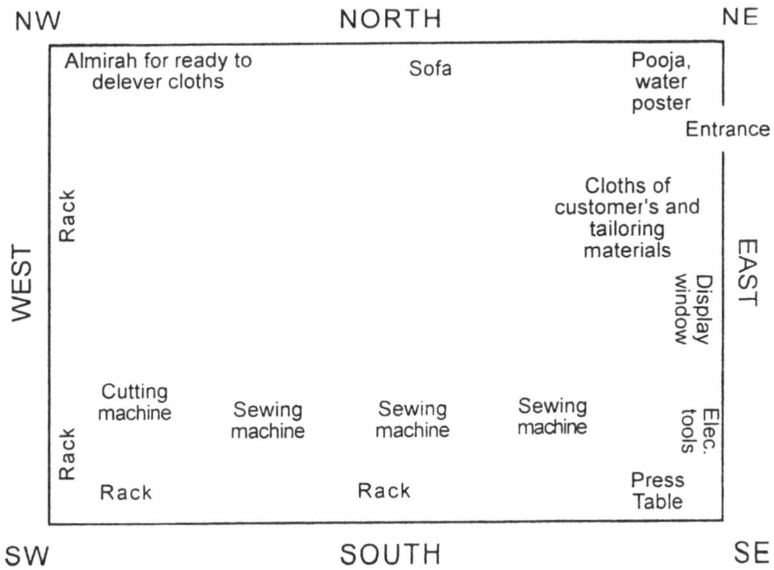

Boutique as per Vaastu

JEWELLERY SHOP AND VAASTU

Attraction for gold, silver and other jewellery in the ladies, is a known fact from the beginning. These are an integral part of their makeup and improve their personality. The jewellery creates a sort of financial security in addition to improve the personality of the ladies. That's why ladies of all the class are always willing to purchase jewellery. In view of this attraction of the ladies for the jewellery there are many big showrooms in almost all the cities.

The jewellery shop earns name and fame both if constructed as per Vaastu:

- The shop for the jewellery should be square or rectangular. It should never be irregular in shape.
- Main entrance of the shop should be in the east of the northeast zone, south of the southeast zone, west of the northwest zone or north of the northeast zone. It should never be in the east of the southeast zone, south, west of the southwest zone or north of the northwest zone.
- The floor of the shop should be either even or lower in the north, east and northeast zone and higher in the south, west and southwest zone.
- The place for worship and drinking water should be in the northeast zone.
- A mirror should be placed on the south or west wall of the shop where the customer can try their look with the jewellery.
- The safe for jewellery should be kept with south or west wall in such a way that it opens in the north or east direction. Do not put the photograph of any God on it.

- The display counters should be in the south or west direction. The sales men should face north or east and the customers west or south direction while sitting.
- Sofa set for the waiting customers maybe in the north or east direction.
- Display window for the jewellery should be in the east or north direction.
- The shop can be painted with any colour other than the yellow.
- The place for packing material should be in the northwest zone.
- The weighing machine for the jewellery should be in the south, west or southwest zone.
- The cash box of the shop should be kept with south wall in such a way that it opens in the north direction.
- Posters and photographs of the jewellery should be placed in the northeast zone.

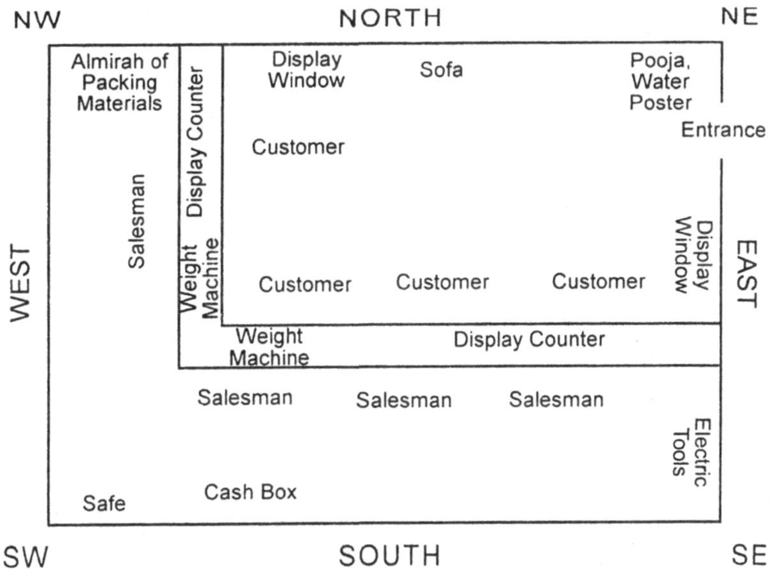

Jewellery shop as per Vaastu

COSMETIC- GENERAL STORE AND VAASTU

Every woman has a natural desire to look beautiful. She applies many types of beautification items on her body no matter how beautiful she is. Natural beautification items were used in old times also. Many new chemical beautification items are in the market these days. Attractive showrooms are constructed to sell these items. The owners of these show rooms earn money and name both if they are constructed as per Vaastu:

- The shop should be square or rectangular in shape. It should never be of irregular shape.
- The main entrance of the store should be in the east of the northeast zone, south of the southeast zone, west of the northwest zone or north of the northeast zone. It should never be in the east of the southeast zone, south, west of the southwest zone or north of the northwest zone.
- The floor of the store should be either even or lower in the north, east and northeast zone and higher in the south, west and southwest zone.
- The place for worship and drinking water should be in the northeast zone only.
- Higher racks for heavy items should be in the south and west and lower racks for light items in the north and east directions.
- The display counter of the store should be in the south or west direction where the salesmen should face north or east and the customer face south or west while sitting.
- Sitting arrangement for the waiting customers can be made in the north or east direction.
- Display window can be in the east or north direction.

- The store should be painted with light green, pink, white or multi colour as per Vaastu.
- A cabin can be constructed in the south or west direction of the store to keep excessive stock.
- Never construct a basement to keep the material in the store. It can be constructed in the north, east or northeast zone, if unavoidable.
- The cash box of the store should be kept along with the south wall in such a way that it opens in the north direction.
- The cosmetics should be kept in the southeast zone, if there is only one counter.
- Seasonal items such, as woolen material in winters and umbrella in the rains etc. should be kept in the northwest zone for fast sells.
- The northeast zone of the shop should always be kept empty because the items kept in this direction are sold slowly. This may cause a loss.
- The arrangement for all the electrical items such as, meter and inverter should be in the southeast zone.

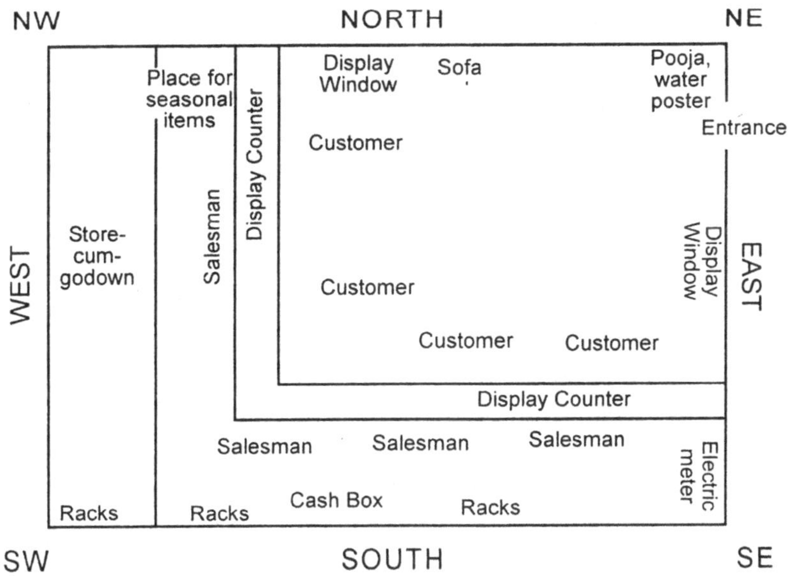

General store as per Vaastu

VAASTU QUESTION-ANSWERS

Q. : I am 30 years old. Do not have mental peace due to divorce. Is the Vaastu of my house not appropriate?

Ans. : It seems that the angle between your house and northeast zone of compound wall is more than 90^0. This defect is the main cause of divorce in many families.

Q. : My son has left the house and living elsewhere in the city just 3 months after his marriage. Health of my wife and mine is also not good. Does it have any relation with the Vaastu of my house?

Ans. : The west direction of your house must be more open than the east. The floor level of the south and southwest zone must be lower or have a pit. The kitchen must be in the northeast zone.

Q. : My wife is very religious but quarrels without any reason. Why is it so?

Ans. : The place of worship seems to be in your bedroom.

Q. : The family of my father-in-law is very prestigious and wealthy. But they are niggardly in spending money. Can it be due to Vaastu?

Ans. : It seems that the house of your father-in-law is increased in the north of the northeast zone. Those living in such houses are niggardly in spending money in spite of earning handsomely.

Q. : My husband always doubts my character. However, there is no such thing and I love my husband a lot.

Ans. : There must be a washbasin in your bedroom itself. If it is so then your husband will always doubt your character.

Q. : I am facing many problems in the marriage of my

daughter in spite of my faith in God and a lot of *puja*. What should be the reason?

Ans. : It seems that either your worship place is in the bedroom or the way to go there passes through the same.

Q. : **The character of wife is dubious and she is not ready to change.**

Ans. : The size of your bedroom must be bigger than all other rooms of the house and you must have kept your bed in front of the entrance of the bedroom.

Q. : **We are married for the last six years but do not have any children. What must be the reason?**

Ans. : The northeast zone of your house must be covered due to your bedroom being in the same zone. There would not be any window, ventilation or door in east or north direction. There must be more open space in the south direction.

Q. : **I have three girls but no son. Is the Vaastu of my house bad?**

Ans. : The northeast zone of your house must be covered due to your bedroom being in the same zone. There must be more open space in the west direction.

Q. : **My only earning son has separated from the family with in six months of his marriage. Does it have any relation with the Vaastu of my house?**

Ans. : The level of the northeast zone of your plot must be higher than the road level and it must be round. The north of the northwest zone must be covered.

Q. : **The infants of my daughter died within 15 days of her delivery twice. What could be the reason?**

Ans. : It seems that the bedroom of your daughter is in the northeast zone and without any window or door in the same. There must be houses on both the sides of her bedroom. There is no childbirth in such a condition and if the children are born they do not live long.

Q. : **We brought up our only girl fondling. She seems**

less affectionate to us after her marriage while we are dying to meet her. Why so?

Ans. : There must be more open space in the south than in the north of your house.

Q. : Our son has separated from us just after his marriage and has almost lost affection to us. Can it be due to Vaastu defects?

Ans. : Yes. There must be more open space in the west direction than the east direction of your house.

Q. : Is Vaastu helpful in the timely marriage of the children?

Ans. : Yes, it is. It can be proved that those living in the houses as per Vaastu lived systematic life and their children got married in time.

Q. : My 19 years old girl married her boy friend against our wishes in Arya Samaj Temple. Is it due to the Vaastu of my house?

Ans. : Yes. It seems that the bedroom of your girl is in the northwest zone of the house and is lower due to some reason.

Q. : There are many marriage proposals for my 28 years old elder sister. But we are not able to finalise any one due to some reasons. Is there a Vaastu defect in our house?

Ans. : Yes. The bedroom of your sister must be in the southwest zone. Advise her to sleep in a bedroom of northwest zone and to keep bed in such a way that it could be used from both sides.

Q. : I am doing B. Com. I cannot concentrate on my studies. I am always in tension. What maybe the reason? Please advise.

Ans. : It seems that you study beneath a beam. Change the place of your study. Do your studies facing east.

Q. : My children cannot study systematically due to bad financial condition. What should I do?

Ans. : This maybe due to higher northeast zone of your house. Get it corrected.

Q. : My son has left the house as he was lagging in the studies. Is it due to bad Vaastu?

Ans. : The ceiling of the room in the northeast zone of your house must be high than other rooms.

Q. : My son and me are not able to get a suitable job. This disrupts the peace of the family. Is there a Vaastu defect in my house?

Ans. : There must be more open space in the south or west of your house than in the north or east direction. The northeast zone of your house must be covered due to a toilet or bathroom.

Q. : My son is mentally retarded and is being treated for the same. Can his condition improve if live in a house as per Vaastu?

Ans. : Yes. Please continue his treatment without any carelessness. It is true that houses with more open space in north and east, slope in north and east, entrance in northeast zone and underground water source in northeast zone help improving mentally retarded children.

VAASTU PROBLEMS AND SOLUTIONS

My readers regularly write to me about their Vaastu related problems after going through my articles in the famous magazine of India *'Grihlaxmi'*. I am going to describe some of them below. You can solve your problems of Vaastu after reading these and observing your own commercial and residential places.

Special: I have suggested solutions on the basis of the maps sent to me by the readers. Most of the readers send maps with all the details regarding the length, breadth, main entrance, doors, windows, drawing room, kitchen, toilets, bathroom, underground water sources etc. of the house. The detail of the floor level, which is a significant part of Vaastu, is not given. Mind you this should never be neglected when Vaastu analysis is done.

PROBLEM: We are facing scarcity after shifting to new house. Income is all right but savings are nil. We are not happy at home. Marriage proposals of my brother and my are also not getting through.

–Rupali, Gamharia

SOLUTION: The toilet and bathroom of your house are in the northeast zone. Construct them any where in the centre of north or centre of east. Construct an underground water tank in this place. This will solve most of your problems.

Sleep in the bedroom no. 3 for marriage soon. Shift your parents in the bedroom no.2 and your brother in the bedroom no. 1. Keep the beds in bedroom nos. 1and 2 with south and

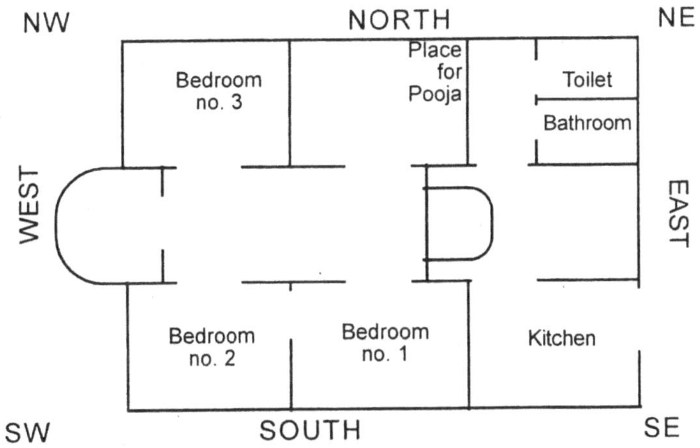

Map of Rupali's house

in no.1 with west wall in such a way that they could be used from all three sides.

These changes will solve all your problems.

PROBLEM: We always quarrel due to lack of coordination. My husband remains mentally upset and cannot concentrate on anything. This all is affecting children adversely.

–Balbir Kaur, Amritsar

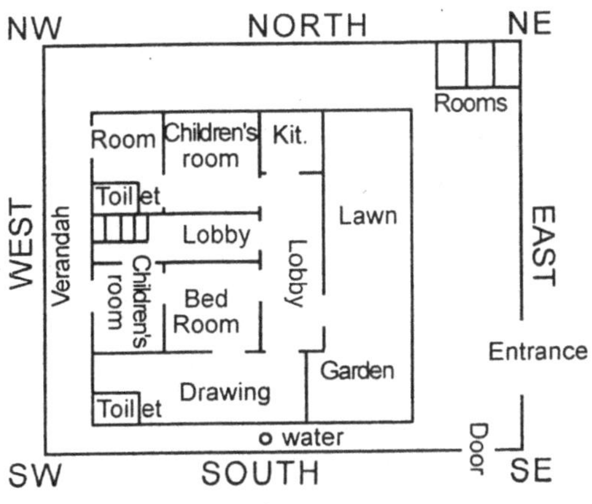

Map of Balbir Kaur's house

SOLUTION: You have constructed rooms in the northeast zone, which has covered the same. It is a significant Vaastu defect. Demolish these rooms. Keeping this place empty is auspicious as per vaastu.

Close underground water source in the south, by soil filling. The ladies of house face physical and mental problems due to underground water source in the south direction. Construct this in the northeast zone on the place of the demolished rooms. It will benefit you.

Main entrance is also in the southeast zone. This is the main cause of lack of coordination and quarrel. Construct your main entrance in the east of the southeast zone or south of the southeast zone.

Shift your kitchen in the southeast zone and construct a lobby and entrance in place of existing kitchen in the northeast zone.

All these changes will be helpful in solving your problems.

PROBLEM: Family tension is increasing, mental peace is disturbed, we doubt each other, financial condition is also not good and cannot save money, since we have constructed and shifted in our new house.

–Jaidev Singh, Pori, Garhwal

SOLUTION: Following Vaastu defects are the cause of your problems:

Main entrance is in the west of the southwest, boring in the south direction, and toilet/bathroom in the northeast zone and more open space in the west direction. All these are significant Vaastu defects, which cannot be corrected without demolition.

East direction of your house will become equally open to the west of your house, if you demolish the toilet/bathroom of northeast zone and kitchen of east of the southeast zone. Fill the boring of south direction. Shift the boring in the northeast zone on the place of toilet/bathroom. You can construct kitchen and toilet/bathroom in the place of bedroom.

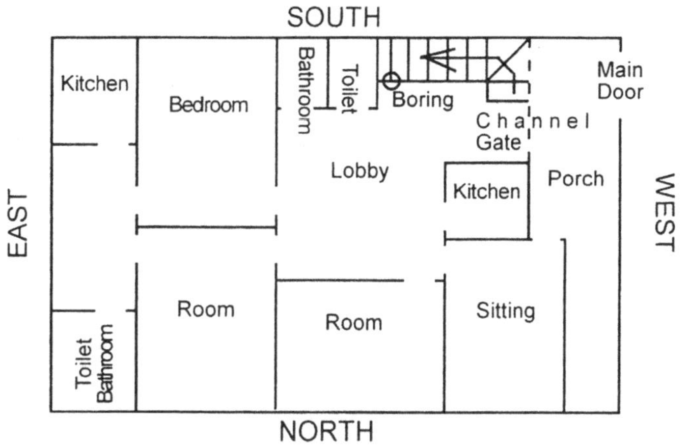

Map of Jaidev Singh's house

Shift the main entrance from west of the southwest to west of the northwest zone. Close the channel gate. Close the door in south of the southwest zone of the drawing room. Use the door in west of the southwest frequently.

I believe that making these changes will solve most of your problems. No other alternative like *puja*, charm or pyramid will be useful in place of this demolition.

PROBLEM: Both of us are in tension. We have quarrels in the house, husband suffers from skin disease and every body at home is ill and a lot of expenses in the house. We always get bad name. Where should we construct the study room for the children?

–Smt. Manju Singh, Agra (UP)

SOLUTION: Entrance of the boundary wall of your house is in west of the southwest zone. This brings financial, mental and physical problems to the males of the house. Shift this door in west of the northwest zone.

Main entrance of the house is also in west of the southwest zone. Shift this too in west of the northwest zone. One door of bedroom is in front of the main entrance in west of the

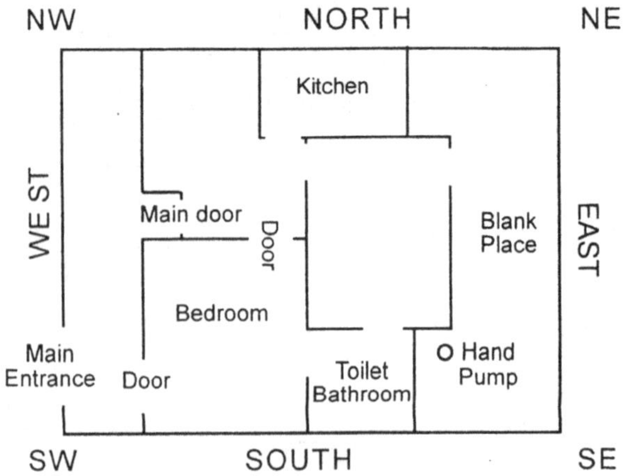

Map of Smt. Manju Singh's house

southwest zone. Shift this also in the west of the northwest zone.

Hand pump in southeast zone is the cause of quarrels in the house. Close this pump and make a new pump in the east of the northeast zone. This will improve the financial, mental and physical condition of the family.

Kitchen in the northeast zone is the cause of mental unrest. Shift this in east of the southeast zone. This will decrease mental unrest.

Your plot is quite good but the construction is erroneous. All the four angles of boundary wall are of 90^0. The north-east zone is depressed due to the room near kitchen. This has also depressed the northeast zone of boundary wall. It inauspicious to have a cut, depressed or round northeast zone. Hence make this equal to the room so that northeast zone is not depressed.

It will be as per Vaastu to construct the rooms for children above the bedroom.

PROBLEM: We are not getting anything straight, cannot save money, beauty parlour is not running well, younger sister is not able to concentrate in studies and we all three sisters are not well since we have shifted to this new flat.

–Jyotsana, Andheri (Mumbai)

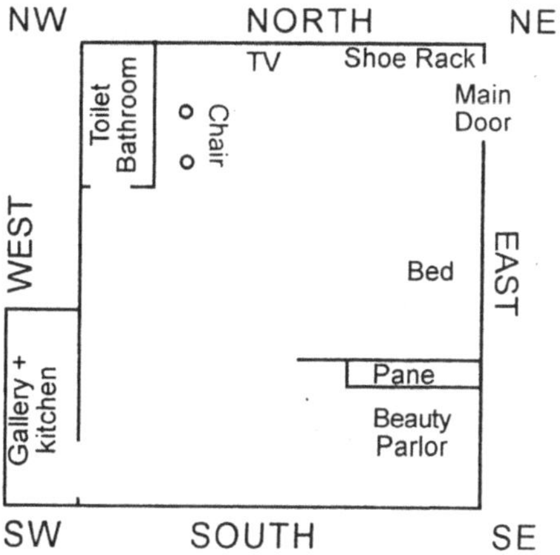

Map of Jyotsana's house

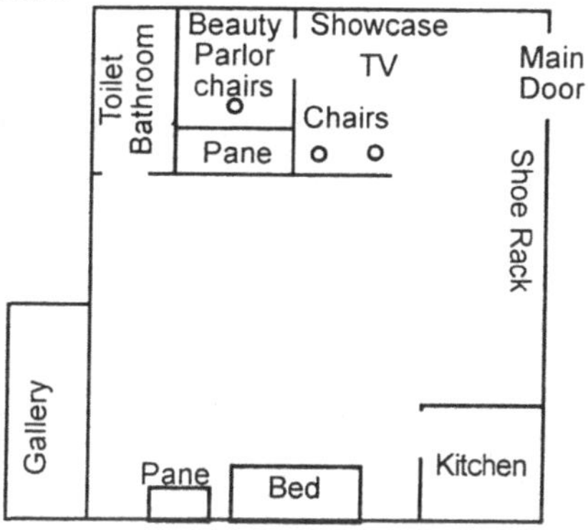

Corrected map

SOLUTION: West of the southwest zone of your room, where kitchen is situated, is increased due to gallery. Placement of furniture of your house is also not as per Vaastu.

You can get relief by closing the part of gallery with plywood, not keeping any type of stuff in gallery and treating the gallery as if it were not a part of your house as per the corrected map. If the interior is done as per the corrected map you will certainly get relief from the problems.

PROBLEM: Tension between husband and wife. There is uncertainty in business, job and income is also insufficient.

–Sharad Joshi, Pune (Maharashtra)

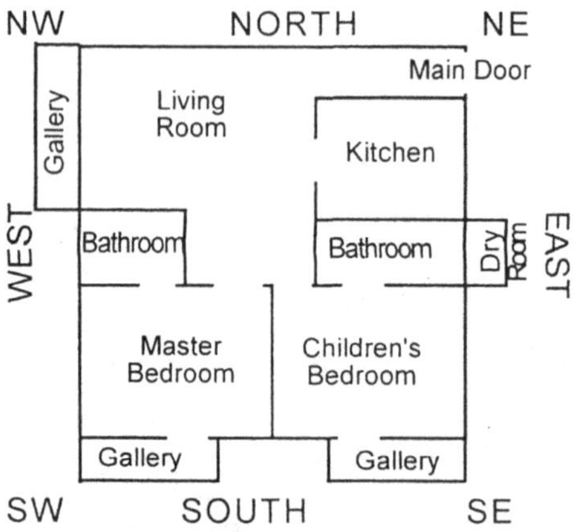

Map of Sharad Joshi's house

SOLUTION: Use water in the direction of wall in north on the kitchen platform. Keep hearth and microwave oven in the east direction of kitchen platform with wall in south.

Northeast zone of the flat is depressed due to construction of drawing room in the east direction. It will be better to demolish this construction. Otherwise close the increased part of the drawing room completely. Close the door with plywood or by a wall and do not keep any thing there. Treat this area as if it were not a part of your flat. I believe that these changes will benefit you.

PROBLEM: There is always difference of opinion among the family members. lack of happy married life, quarrel in the family and disturbed peace. However, all the family members are simple by nature.

–Sudhanshu Sharma, Moradabad, (UP)

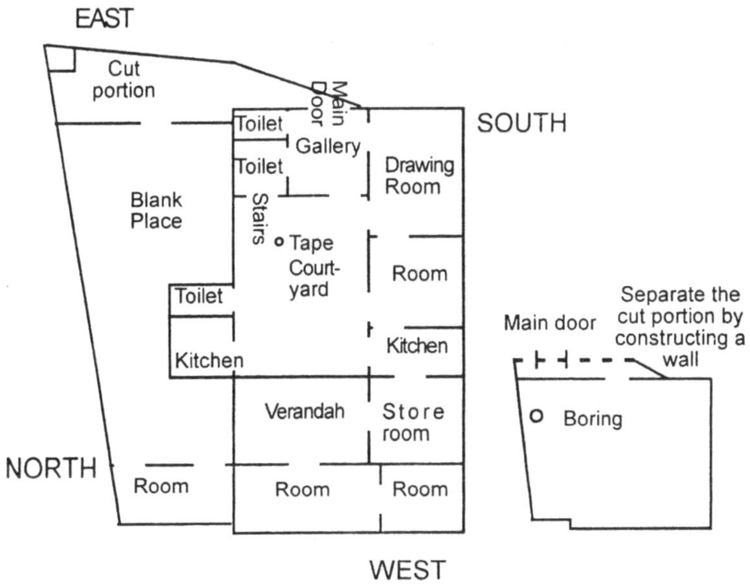

Map of Sudhanshu Sharma's house

SOLUTION: The shape of your plot is auspicious but a cut in the east direction has created a significant Vaastu defect in the same. Remove this defect by constructing a wall in the east direction, as shown in the corrected map. Most of problems will be solved.

The main entrance of the house is in southeast zone right now. This is the cause behind difference of opinion in the family. Shift this in east of the northeast zone. This auspicious change will solve your problem.

Removal of above two defects will solve almost 80% of problems.

Your life will become very smooth if you create an underground water source such as water tank, boring or well in the northeast zone.

You will have to demolish a lot of construction to remove the rest of the 20% defects, which is not needed at the moment.

PROBLEM: We have shifted to this house recently. In which direction the children should study and tell us the way to remove the Vaastu defects, if any.

–Ms. Priyanka, Muzaffarnagar, (UP)

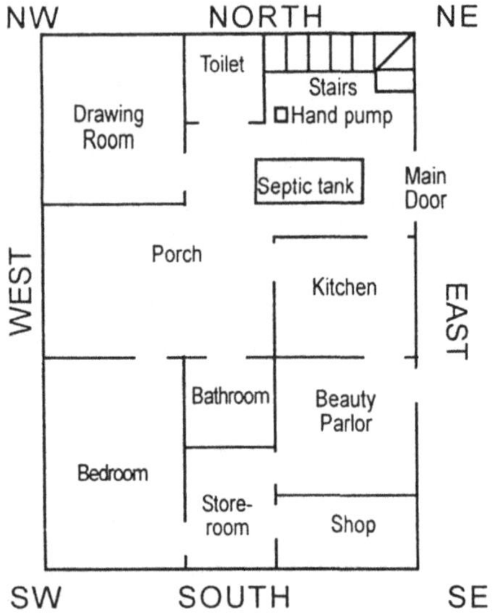

Map of Ms. Priyanka's house

SOLUTION: There are some Vaastu defects in your house, which will manifest their effect within some time. You should get these changes done in your house for happy future.

The septic tank of your house is in wrong place. This will create physical, mental and financial problems for you. Close it completely and make the septic tank below the toilet.

Your hand pump is in right position. But constructing a small fresh water tank near the staircase will strengthen your financial condition further.

Door of the drawing room is in east of the southeast zone right now. Shift this in south of the southeast zone.

It will be as per Vaastu for the children to do their studies in the bedroom in the southwest zone or drawing room in the northwest zone. They should face east while studying.

PROBLEM: In our family we unnecessarily exchange words among one another. My younger son is not interested in studies. Elder son does not work or any job properly. Please explain the "Horseshoe" and "Quartz Circle".

–Smt. Lakshmikanta, Alwalpur (Punjab)

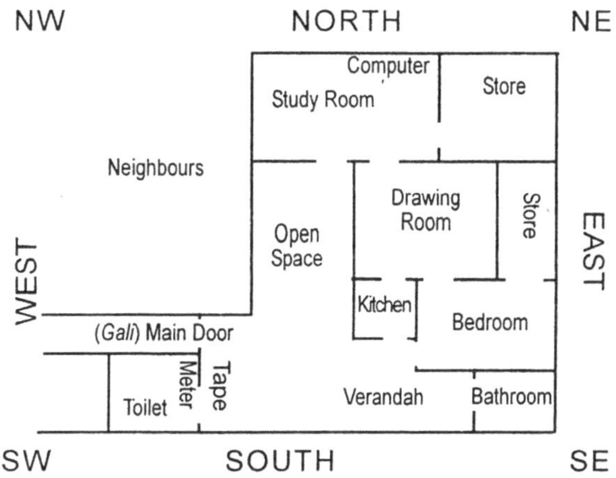

Map of Smt. Lakshmikanta's house

SOLUTION: Following Vaastu defects are responsible for all the problems of your house.

The southwest zone of your house is increased. Main entrance of your house is also from the same direction in a *gali*. There is a store in the northeast zone. South, west and southwest zone are open. All these are against Vaastu. It will be better for you to leave this place and shift in another house for happy future. It is impossible for you to change the entrance of the house.

If there is negative energy in a room, the "Quartz Circles" remove it and make the room full of energy. To save the house from evil eye, "Horseshoe" is put in the inverted "U" shape on the entrance but this will not make any difference in your case.

PROBLEM: My children are still unmarried. All the three are of 34, 26 and 24 years of age respectively. 34 Years old son is still not settled in business. Please suggest me some solution. *– Shri Pramod Shah, Mulund*

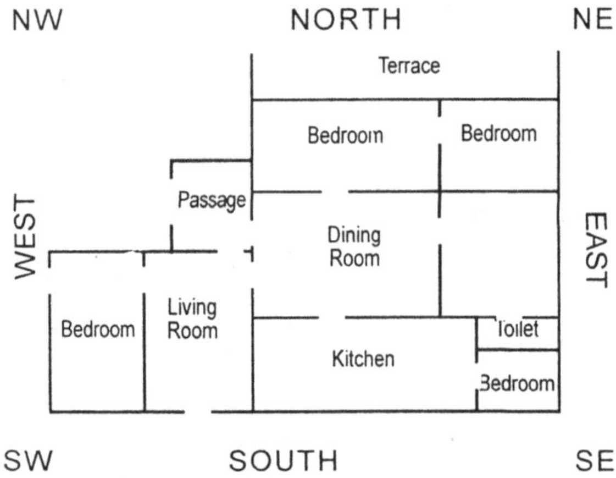

Map of Shri Pramod Shah's house

SOLUTION: Following Vaastu defect is the cause of your problem:

West of the southwest zone of your irregularly constructed flat is increased. This causes mental and financial troubles for the men of the family, which is the case in your family too. There is no possibility of any improvement in the Vaastu of this flat. It will be better for you to shift somewhere else for good future.

PROBLEM: I am not able to achieve any post or prestige. I am always under mental pressure and feel physical weakness. My wife is also stressed and weak. We seek a son. Our three years old daughter is also very stubborn in nature. Whether my house is auspicious or not, as per Vaastu? Please inform.

–Shri Sawai Singh, Jaipur (Rajasthan)

SOLUTION: Following Vaastu defects in your house are the cause for your problems:

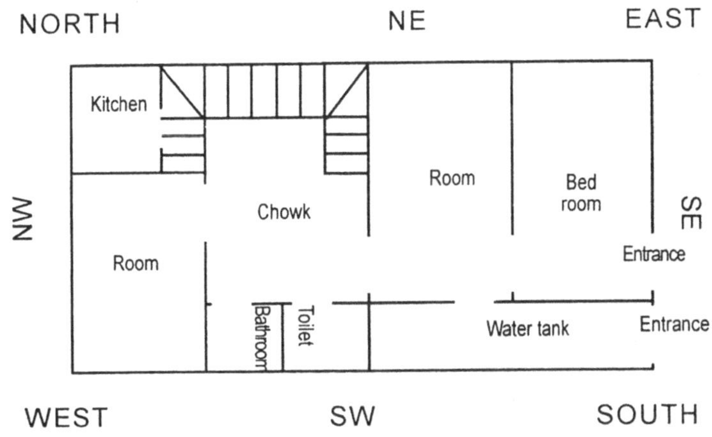

Map of Shri Sawai Singh's house

All the doors of your house, including the main entrance, are in the south direction. There is a water tank inside the house opposite main entrance in southwest zone. Staircase is in the northeast zone. Kitchen is in the north direction.

You should shift all the doors from south to east direction in the front. Demolish the staircase and construct the same in the southwest zone near toilet. Construct the water tank, where there is kitchen right now and construct the kitchen in the place of water tank. Construct overhead tank for water above the toilet bathroom.

These changes may solve your problems.

PROBLEM: Our financial condition is very bad. My parents are always ill. No guest feels comfortable in our house.

–Shri Jagannath Yadav, Patna (Bihar)

SOLUTION: Cut northeast zone is the most significant Vaastu defect of your house. There is only one solution for this, either do construction as suggested in the corrected map and level it with kitchen or demolish kitchen and courtyard both. You can construct here a temple also, if you like. Your

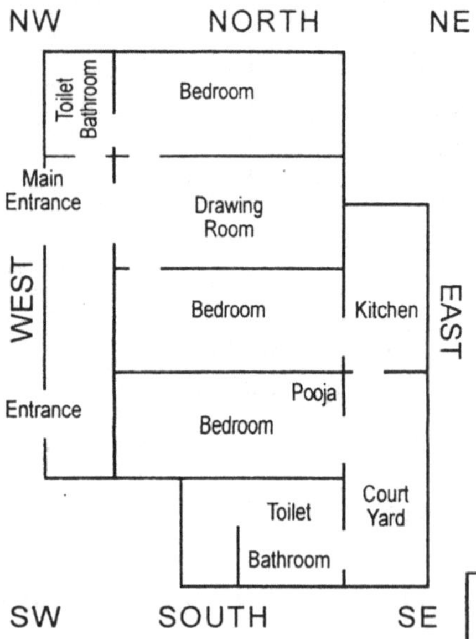

Map of Shri Jagannath Yadav's house

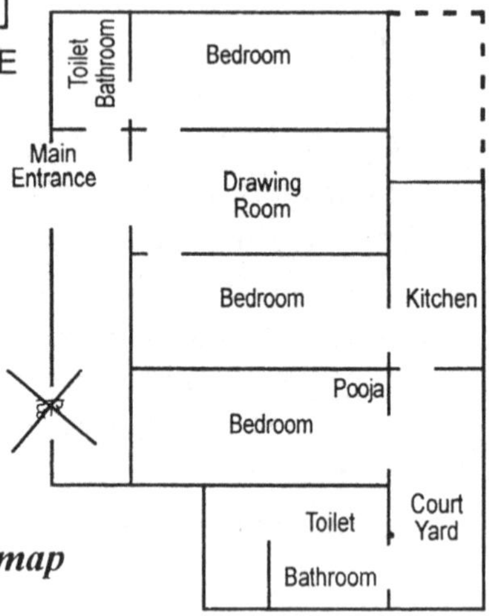

Corrected map

bad financial condition is due to this reason only and your son is also suffering due to this defect only.

The doors of your study room and bedroom are also in wrong direction and hence not usable. Correct them as per the map.

Construct a commode on a platform, if the seat of the toilet, in the south, is either of Indian style or commode is fitted in a pit on the floor.

Any pit in the south direction creates bad financial condition and bad health. These changes will definitely improve your condition.

PROBLEM: We always face loss of money and health problems in this house. We do not have any child. We are on the verge of a disaster. Please suggest us solution.

–Shri Gajaendra Singh, Rewaria (Rajasthan)

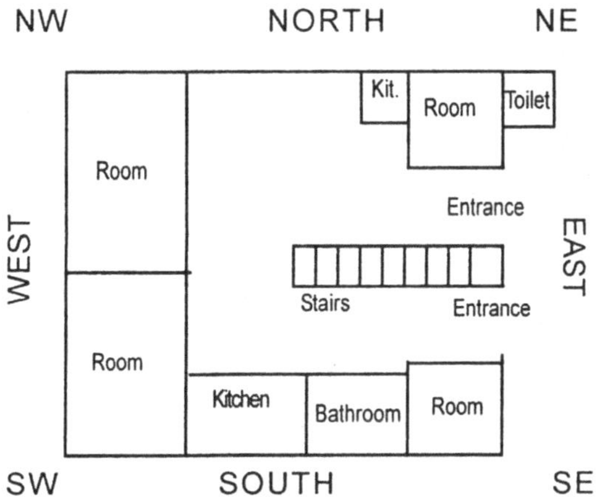

Map of Shri Gajendra Singh's house

SOLUTION: As per the map of your house the construction is not correct. Toilet in the northeast zone is inauspicious. It creates many troubles. But quantum your problems suggest to me that your house has more than this defect only. For example there may be higher east and northeast zone than the west and southwest zone, a pit in the centre or a septic tank in the southwest zone. I can guess about such defects because whatever you have described in your problems is not shown in the map as defects.

Even then you demolish the toilet of the northeast zone and construct the same in the north direction near the kitchen. Definitely you will have some benefit.

PROBLEM: Can we shift our kitchen, which is in the northeast zone at present, to the *puja* room of our flat? Please suggest us other changes also to make the family happy.

–Smt. Radhika, Jamshedpur (Bihar)

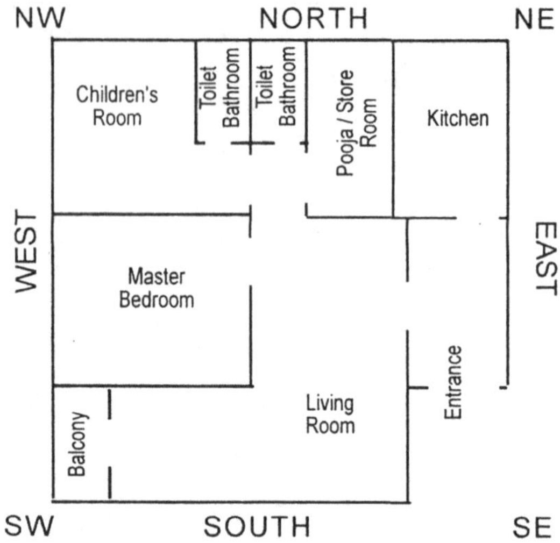

Map of Smt. Radhika's house

SOLUTION: A thorough reading of the map of your flat reveals that it is constructed almost as per Vaastu. Such flats are rare.

It is better to shift your kitchen of northeast zone in the *puja* room but it will be best to shift the same in northwest in the children's room. Shift the room of children in the place of kitchen. Keep their table and chair in such a way that they face east while studying.

PROBLEM: We constructed our house in the year 1993-94 but shifted there in April 2001. We are facing many problems since then. We are all perturbed due to illness and especially I am very much disturbed. Please help us to over come the problems.

–Shri Jeevan Singh, Madhepura

SOLUTION: The plot on which your house is situated, is very auspicious. Main entrance in the south of the southeast and hand pump in the east of the northeast is also in proper places. But there is some Vaastu defect due to some wrong constructions and this has caused the problems for your whole family.

Vaastu defects and their corrections are as below:

1. Septic tank near the hand pump is almost in the east of the northeast zone. This causes ill health of the family members. Close it by soil filling and construct it as shown in the corrected map.

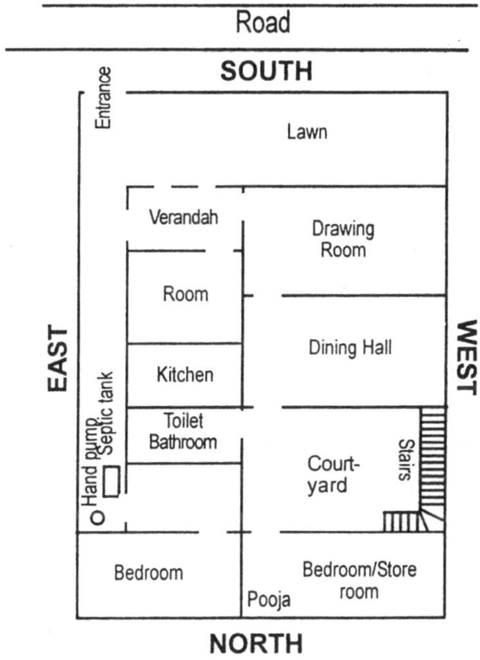

Map of Shri Jeevan Singh's house

2. Northeast zone of your house is covered due to bedroom. Reduce this bedroom in the northeast zone, as shown in the corrected map and increase the courtyard.
3. South direction of the house is open and north is covered

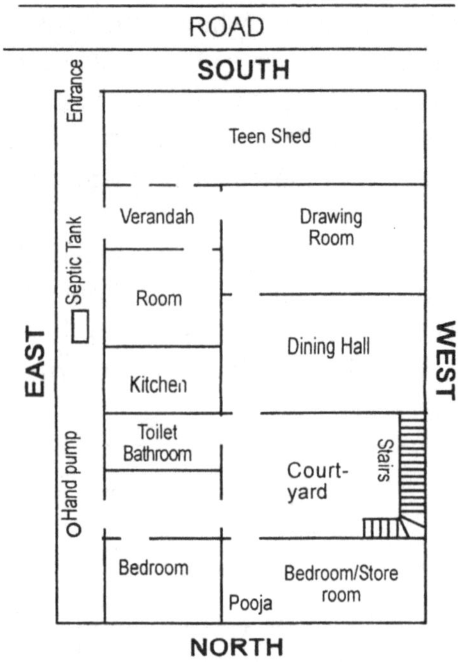

Corrected Map of Shri Jeevan Singh's house

due to bedroom. Hence some construction is required in the south direction too. You can cover the lawn of the south direction, by a plastic or tin shade. The height of this shade should be equal to the roof of the ground floor. I hope that these changes will make your future happy.

SOLUTIONS TO VAASTU QUERIES

Q.1 : Is Vaastushaastra for the followers of Hinduism?

Ans. : No. The Indian *rishis* and *munis* invented Vaastushaastra for all those living on the earth. It is equally applicable to all belonging to any religion, cult or breed.

Q.2 : The earth encircles the sun and spins on its own axis, i.e. it is not stable. What is the utility of Vaastu in such a condition?

Ans. : It is right that the earth revolves on its axis and encircles the sun too. Our whole universe is also running towards infinite in the Milky Way very fast. Many carriages of a train run on the rail simultaneously. All the luggage in the carriages is stable while they are in motion. If suddenly the speed is either reduced or increased the luggage is disturbed. Similarly, the earth is also revolving on its axis with a uniform speed from the beginning. All the fixed things on its surface are stable. The basis of the Vaastushaastra is omnipresent five elements, viz. earth, water, fire, air and sky. To construct a house and decorate it as per these five elements is called Vaastu.

Q.3 : How does a layman know whether his house is as per Vaastu or not?

Ans. : Suppose your life is smooth, peaceful and business is good. When you change the residence and life becomes miserable, peace is disturbed, loss in business, face health problems then it clearly suggests that the new house or renovation of old one is not as per Vaastu.

Q-4 : If in spite of Vaastu defects life is happy and peaceful even than the removal of Vaastu defects is required?

Ans. : No. It is true that when the fortune is favourable and strong Vaastu defects are not felt. But when the fortune is not favourable then Vaastu defects become strong and disrupt the life. As long as fortune is favourable there is no need to make any changes in Vaastu. We visit our doctor only when we fall ill. A healthy person does not go to see his doctor. When day to day life is disturbed then only the removal of the Vaastu defects should be done.

Q-5 : Does Vaastu affect men and women separately?

Ans. : Yes. As per Vaastu east of the north east, north of the north-east, west of the north-west and west of the south-west represent region of man. South-east, south, south of the south-west and north of the north-west represent woman. All the other directions of Vaastu affect them equally.

Q-6 : Do east-facing or north-facing plots are as per Vaastu?

Ans. : No. All the four directions are natural. Construction can be carried out facing any one direction as per Vaastu. But as per Vaastu much open space should be left in the north and east directions to get more advantage of morning vital sun rays. Less open space should be left in the south and west directions to avoid contact with the negative rays of the sun afternoon. That's why there is no ample parking space in front of the south and west facing houses. East and north-facing plots are therefore rated better.

Q-7 : Is Vaastu applicable to the residents of ground floor only?

Ans. : Residents of ground floor are affected by Vaastu 100% because this is related to the earth. Underground water source, gardens, main gate, high and low of the ground and shape of the ground are all on the earth. The effect of the earth on Vaastu decreases as the height increases. It is only 80 to 90% effective on 8th-9th floor approximate.

Q-8 : Can Vaastu defects be eradicated by the Chinese Vaastushaastra–Feng Shui?

Ans. : Yes. Principle of the Feng Shui says that if there is a problem there is solution. But it is applicable to eradicate very small Vaastu defects only.

Q-9 : What is the similarity between Indian Vaastushaastra and Chinese Feng Shui ?

Ans. : There are different systems of medicine, e.g. Ayurved, Allopathy, Homeopathy and Unani etc. with only one aim, i.e. to keep the human being healthy. Similarly, Indian Vaastushaastra and Feng Shui are the old art of coordinating between shape, proportion and direction of a building, its surroundings with the environment.

Q-10: Are the principles of Vaastushaastra and Feng Shui applicable in India and China only respectively?

Ans. : No. The principles of Vaastushaastra and Feng Shui are based on the sun rays and magnetic rays flowing on the earth, which are not affected by man-made borders of the countries.

Q-11: Can Vaasushaastra and Feng Shui both be applied simultaneously in one Vaastu?

Ans. : Yes. The simultaneous application of Vaastushaastra and Feng Shui is much advantageous. Both should be applied under the advice of experienced and learned Vaastu consultants.

Q-12: How does Vaastu affect more than one property of the same person?

Ans. : If a person owns more than one properties then the Vaastu of property he uses for his residence and business purposes affects his life. The property, which he has given to others, will affect its users. If a property, which is not in any use affects the owner only.

Q-13: How does Vaastu affect more than one business premises of the same person?

Ans. : If a businessman possesses more than one business premises, then he will enjoy all the advantages of the business premises which is as per Vaastu. But He will have to face the disadvantages of all the Vaastu defects present in other business premises.

Q-14: In our country houses are small. Maximum people live in such houses where one or two rooms are shared by all the family members. In such a case what should be the solution?

Ans. : It is auspicious to decorate a small house or one room house treating it as single Vaastu as per Vaastu, i.e in the south-east region of the room hearth should be kept, water should be kept in the north-east angle and almirah should be kept in the south-west zone.

Please read article entitled "Interior Decoration of One Rcom and Vaastu" in the book *"Interior Decoration Vaastu and Feng Shui"* by this author.

Q-15: Young family member goes out of the house, in other city to study. Will the Vaastu defects of his house affect his career?

Ans. : No. Wherever that young person lives in other city the Vaastu of that place or room will affect his career.

Q-16: Does tying a cow or planting *tulsi* in front of the house eradicate Vaastu defects?

Ans. : Not at all. Due to its utility the cow is treated as mother. To tie cow, to apply the cow dung on the courtyard and to wash the house with cow urine are all our religious faiths. Similarly, due to its medicinal properties *tulsi* is worshipped. This is also our religious faith. Vaastushaastra is a science. Hence there is no advantage in applying any religious faith to eradicate Vaastu defects.

Q-17: In a house constructed as per Vaastu, can Vaastu defect originate per se?

Ans. : Many changes occur around us on their own. These sometimes create Vaastu defects even in a house constructed as per Vaastu. For example, small plants in the north-east zone of a house when grow become big trees then they start obstructing vital morning sun rays. It becomes a significant Vaastu defect.

If a highway or a bridge is constructed in the north or east and a big drain is constructed in the south or west of the house it creates a Vaastu defect. So there are many factors that may create Vaastu defect in a house constructed as per Vaastu.

Q-18: Is there any use of erecting Vaastu defect prevention machine?

Ans. : Not at all. There is no mention of any such machine in any book published on Vaastushaastra from the first book to any book till 1995. This Vaastu defects prevention machine has been invented by some greedy Vaastu consultants to plunder innocent people. It is created by charging very high price. It does not give even 1% relief.

Q-19: Is there any machine available to search Vaastu defects?

Ans. : No. The *rishi-munis*, who invented Vaastushaastra did not create such a machine. There is no description of such a machine in any old Indian or Chinese book. Some Vaastu consultants use "Lacquer Antenna" machine to detect Vaastu defects. By doing so they simply plunder people as this machine is basically used to measure energy of environment and human system.

Q-20: Can we eradicate Vaastu defects ourselves by merely reading a few books on the subject?

Ans. : No. Vaastushaastra seems very easy while reading but very difficult when applied. Only a few general Vaastu defects can be removed by reading some books but significant Vaastu defects can not be eradicated. People with shallow knowledge can not even differentiate between general and significant Vaastu defect. Hence it is recommended to consult an able and learned Vaastu consultant.

EPILOGUE

I have written 8 books on various aspects of Vaastu and Feng Shui, after gaining experience from successful Vaastu consultancy for years. I have written these books to facilitate you to construct or alter your residence or office as per Vaastu to lead a happy, peaceful and prosperous life.

I have experienced that in any corner of the world, if somebody is successful in any field of the life, his residence or office is as per Vaastu. If there is even a small Vaastu defect then that person has to suffer from the consequences of the same.

Common people have illusion that it is very costly to construct home as per Vaastu and its waste of space also. But it is completely wrong. In fact, it is very economical to construct home as per Vasstu and no space is wasted. Every inch of the space available is utilized in right ways. A small house, constructed as per Vaastu looks big and specious.

I have described various principles in my books to take full advantage of Vaastu. If you are unable to follow them though I request you to follow only three important principles, as follows, to make your life happy and successful. These three principles are of significance as if they are compulsory question of 20 marks each in a question paper of 100 marks. All other principles bear only 1-2 marks. One point is to be made clear in this example that if there is anyone wrong answer the marking will then be negative.

1. North-east zone of any plot or building should never be covered, compressed, cut, deducted, or round. The south-west zone should not be raised.

2. Underground water source e.g. well, bore-well, tank, septic tank etc. or any other hole and any slope should only be in north, north-east or east direction. Never construct septic tank in north-east zone. It should be constructed in north or east direction only.
3. Boundary wall and main gate of the building can be in east of the north-east, south of the south-east, west of the north-west and north of the north-east.

Special

Under no circumstances the entrance gate should be in south of the south-west or west of the south-west.

If these three principles are followed, believe me, your Vaastu will be in grade I.

If in any building there is anyone of the above mentioned Vaastu defect then it is certain that the life of the residents will not be happy. Maybe due to strong fortune he may not feel the impact but the moment his fortune becomes weak, horrible problems will come in his life.

Above mentioned Vaastu defects can not be corrected with out destroying old construction. It is sheer waste of money and time to use pyramid, Shree Yantra, wind chime, crystal ball or other Feng Shui material, perform the *puja* for peace of Vaastu, stick craft, use *yantra, tantra* and *mantra* to correct these Vaastu defects.

Consult an able and experienced Vaastu consultant if you are suffering from Vaastu defects or want to construct a new building. Do not hesitate to pay proper fees to a good Vaastu consultant. I would like to draw your attention to the fact that a true and able consultant may charge high for his services. He gives you advice only and not pyramid, *yantra* or any other stuff. But the advantage of his advice is thousand times valuable than the fees you pay. Moreover, that advice makes your life happy, peaceful and prosperous.

THE NEBULA INTERNATIONAL SCHOOL OF SCIENTIFIC VAASTU

Vaastu Guru Mr. Kuldeep Saluja, an internationally renowned Vaastu consultant has written 8 books on different aspects of Vaastu and Feng Shui. He has been praised by his readers on international level and has become immensely popular.

Mr. Saluja has established an exclusive identity of his own by his deep study, thinking and research and knowledge of Vaastu, developed by the research work of *rishi* and *munis* for thousand years and Feng Shui a five thousand year old Chinese Vaastu explored by the Chinese intellectuals. He has solved many doubts by question-answer sessions during his various trips to abroad. He is determined to create Vaastu education, students and teachers so as to reach this science to common people. To promote the course of this Vaastu education he has started a correspondence course. This correspondence course will give knowledge of Vaastu to all the keen students. They can take Vaastu as a career and earn money after becoming Vaastu consultants.

Many readers wrote to Mr. Saluja and showed their keen interest to learn Vaastu and to choose it as a career. Respecting this feeling "The Nebula International School of Scientific Vaastu" was established. A correspondence course of international level has been started by the institute. The curriculum has been prepared by Mr. Saluja on the basis of his experience (personal and practical) of 20 – 22 years. It has been prepared in such a way that it will unveil the scientific mysteries of Vaastu and you will be able to solve problems of others easily.

Mr. Saluja is confident that after finishing study of this course students will be able to eradicate Vaastu defects of house, shop, flat, office, marriage premises, factory, industry, farm house, agricultural land, multi-storeyed building and township etc. successfully anywhere in the world.

Correspondence course study material will be dispatched to the students by post. Evaluation of the assignments of the students will be done by Mr. Saluja. Minimum 75% marks are to be obtained. A practical workshop of all the successful students will be organized and the certificates will be distributed. Mr. Saluja will guide students about the practical aspects and other important information will be provided in this workshop. This course can be completed in minimum six to maximum twelve months.

PROCEDURE TO GET ADMISSION IN VAASTU & FENG SHUI COURSE

Those who are keen to take admission in this course, may apply giving their details e.g. name, address, phone no. etc. on a plain paper along with a D.D. of Rs.20000 as fee for the course. The D.D. should be in favour of "The Nebula International School of Scientific Vaastu" payable at Ujjain.

For the foreigners the fee is USD 1000.00. The fee is to be paid in one installment.

The application along with the D.D. can be sent at the following address:

The Nebula International School of Scientific Vaastu

Billoo & Billoo, Freegunj, Ujjain-456010 (M.P.), India

You can contact on the following Nos. to get more information on the course.

Mobile : 09425091601

Phone : 0091-734-2513229, 2520068

Fax : 0091-734-2513842

e-mail : kuldeep@vaastuguru.com

billoo@sancharnet.in

website : www. vaastuguru.com

www.scientificvaastu.com

After the receipt of the application and fee, name will be registered for the course and identity card, syllabus and study material will be sent. The study material will be dispatched through courier from time to time.

VAASTU RELATED CONSULTATION WITH THE AUTHOR

Vaastu Guru Mr. Kuldeep Saluja is an experienced Vaastu consultant and the director of Billoo & Billoo group of business organization, a famous business organization of Ujjain.

It is generally observed that due to small Vaastu defects many construction works remain uncompleted or go through various problems during the course of construction. A family suffers financial, mental and physical problem or some accidents occur in the family, after shifting in a new house. A multi-storeyed building is ready for commercial use and is with all the modern amenities but nobody turns up to purchase. There are many problems in addition to these e.g. suddenly a good going business stops after expansion of shop or new furniture, shops of a new shopping complex are not sold and remain ruined, factory constructed and ready but production not started or production started but factory running in losses. Many such problems arise from time to time.

If you are also in trouble and desire to consult for removal of the Vaastu defects of house, shop, flat, office, marriage premises, factory, industry, farmhouse, agricultural land, shopping complex, multi-storeyed building or township etc. if you want to start a new construction as per Vaastu, then please contact at the following address and telephone no. and fix appointment.

Here it is worth mentioning that Mr. Saluja is a very busy Vaastu consultant. He very frequently visits many countries for Vaastu consultancy, in condition to India and is not easily available.

CONTACT AT

Kuldeep Saluja
The Nebula International School of Scientific Vaastu
Billoo & Billoo, Freeganj, Ujjain - 456 010, (M.P.), INDIA
Mobile : 094250 91601 **Phones :** 0091 - 734 - 2513229, 2520068
Fax : 0091 - 734 - 2513842
e-mail: kuldeep@vaastuguru.com
billoo@sancharnet.in
website : www.vaastuguru.com, www.scientificvaastu.com

Dear Readers,
This book is in your hands. How do you like it? There is every possibility of mistakes in the book. But our endeavour has been to give substantial information on Vaastu. Please do write to me about any mistake or suggestion. I would be highly obliged. I would like to correct it in the next edition. I will wait for your letters.

Kuldeep Saluja

Some books which you will love to read

BOOK OF LOVE

By: Maria Shaw

Find out with this fun guide to love and friendship. What should I wear on a first date? Is Libra a good match with Aries? How can I find out if someone wants to go out with me. Discover how to get answers to all of your relationship questions with Maria Shaw's Book of Love. Easy to use and fun to read, this unique guide to relationships gives you:

* An astro compatibility guide for each sun sign.
* Quick and easy magical how-to's.
* Palm reading tips and techniques.
* Simple formulas for determining love number compatibility.

SPIRITUAL FITNESS

By: Nancy Mramor

The simple exercises and techniques presented in Spiritual Fitness are not tied to any specific spiritual tradition and can be practiced by anyone. They are designed to lead you toward greater contentment in all areas of your life:

* Improve your physical, emotional, and mental health
* Free yourself from negative behaviours that block happiness
* Discover how to find lasting inner peace
* Deepen your spiritual awareness

HOW TO HEAL WITH COLOR

By: Ted Andrews

How to Heal with Color shows you how to use the vibrational effects of color to heal yourself and others. Learn how to:

* Use colors to balance the chakras
* Determine therapeutic colors by muscle testing
* Apply color therapy through touch, projection, breathing, cloth, water, and candles
* Rid yourself of toxins, negativity, and patterns that hinder your life process
* Use the powerful color-healing system of the mystical Qabala to balance and open the psychic centers
* Perform long-distance healing on others

For vibrant physical, emotional, mental, and spiritual health—add color to your life.

THE INSTINCT TO HEAL

By: David Servan-Schreiber

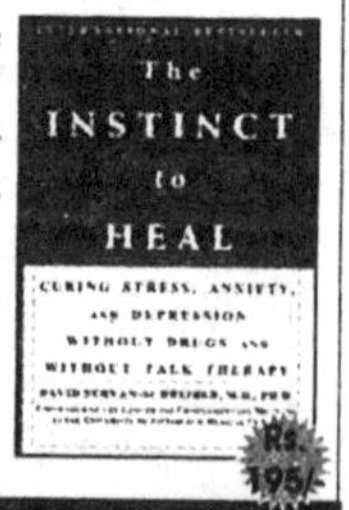

Heal is a powerful word. Isn't it presumptuous for a physician to use such a word in the title of a book on stress, anxiety, and depression? I've thought a lot about this question. To me, "healing" means that patients are no longer suffering from the symptoms that they complained of when they first consulted, and that these symptoms do not come back after the treatment has been completed. This is what happens when we treat an infection with antibiotics. The ideas presented in this book are largely inspired by the works of physicians and researchers.

Fusion Books

X-30, Okhla Industrial Area, Phase-II, New Delhi-110020, Ph.: 41611861, Fax: 41611861,
E-mail: sales@diamondpublication.com, Website: www.diamondpublication.com

Excellent Books On Personality Development

FOR A BETTER TOMORROW

By: Joginder Singh (Former CBI Director)

This magnum opus by Sh. Joginder Singh is a treatise on self improvement. This win-win sotry is based on the secrets of success as to how to become an achiever. And the success mantra that he espouses for you: Make the best of all opportunities; dream big and work hard—dreams will turn sheer realities. You only need to hone your skills and attitude to become a winner.

Price: Rs. 150/-

WHY WOMEN ARE WHAT THEY ARE

By: Swati Lodha

A book which empowers women to command a unique status, dignity and respect for herself. If you are a daughter, wife or a mother this book will hold your hand and guide you. If you are a son, husband or a father, this book will motivate towards perfection in these roles.

Price: Rs. 195/-

COME ON! GET SET GO...

By: Swati-Shailesh Lodha

This book reveals your real self. It tells you about the hairline difference between a person who is a real success and the one who pretends to be so. This book prompts you to discover yourself. This book doesn't make you "The Best" but it makes you "Second to None".

Price: Rs. 195/-

THE EXCELLENCE IN YOU

By: Dr. Giriraj Shah

This book teaches you to do the same manage your life as a whole. It tells you about your aims in life, how sincerity and perseverance help you to achieve those aims. It teaches you how your presence of mind can make you perfect. It also tells you about various etiquettes, and mannerisms to be used in life.

Price: Rs. 150/-

THE SECRET OF HAPPINESS

By: Jas Mand

This book does not endorse any religious methodology to achieved a state of bliss as most religions claim. The author has attempted to approach the subject of happiness from the scientific angle of a rationalist. Unlike self-help books, it does not offer first-aid. It proposes regular and non-stop work on your growth all the time. The basic emphasis is on cultivating the attitude of happiness, which primarily is in one's own hands.

Price: Rs. 195/-

Fusion Books

X-30, Okhla Industrial Area, Phase-II, New Delhi-110020, Ph.: 41611861, Fax: 41611861,
E-mail: sales@diamondpublication.com, Website: www.diamondpublication.com

DIAMOND POCKET BOOKS PRESENTS

ASTROLOGY, VAASTU, PALMISTRY & RELIGION BOOKS

Dr. Bhojraj Dwivedi

Be your own Astrologer

Ascendant Libra 150.00
Ascendant Aries 150.00
Ascendant Taurus 150.00
Ascendant Gemini 150.00
Ascendant Cancer 150.00
Ascendant Leo 150.00
Ascendant Virgo 150.00
Ascendant Scorpio 150.00
Ascendant Sagittarius 150.00
Ascendant Capricorn 150.00
Ascendant Aquarius 150.00
Ascendant Pisces 150.00
*Hindu Traditions and Beliefs :A Scientific Validity (Question & Answer) 150.00
*Hindu Traditions and Beliefs (A Religious Validity) 95.00
*Feng Shui : Chinese Vaastu Shastra 195.00
*Pyramid and Temple Vaastu 195.00
*Yantra, Mantra, Tantra and Occult Science 195.00
*Thumb! The Mirror of Fate 150.00
*Astrology & Wealth (Jyotish Aur Dhyan Yog) 95.00
*Jyotish Aur Rajyog 95.00
*Jyotish and Santan Yog 75.00
*Remedial Vaastushastra 200.00
*Sampuran Vaastushastra 200.00
*Commercial Vaastushastra 200.00
*Environmental Vaastu 150.00
*The Mystique of Gems & Stones (4 colour) 250.00
*Kalsarp Yoga Aur Ghatvivah (in Press) 200.00
*The Mystical of Palmistry 295.00
*Study of Omens 95.00
*The Astrological Analysis of Earthquake 60.00

S.N. Mathur, B. K. Chaturvedi

Hindu Gods and Goddesses 295.00

Er. R. Prasad

Magic of Feng Shui 120.00
Magic of Vaastu Shashtra 120.00

Shashi Kant Oak

*Naadi Prediction 95.00

Manish Verma

*Fast & Festivals of India 95.00

Pt. Gopal Sharma, Dr. D.P. Rao

*Pyramid Power & Vaastu 195.00
*Advance Feng Shui (For Health and Happiness) 195.00
*Sri Sai Science of Griha Vaastu 195.00
*Vaastu and Pyramidal Remidies 195.00

Pt. Gopal Sharma

*Comprehensive Vaastu 75.00
*Wonders of Numbers 95.00

Acharya Vipul Rao

*Hypnotism 95.00

Cheiro

*Cheiro's Language of the Hand (Palmistry) 95.00
*Cheiro's Book of Numerology .. 60.00
*Cheiro's Astro Numerology & Your Star 95.00
*Cheiro's Book of Astrology 95.00

B.R. Chuwdhary

*Speed Palmistry with Memory Tips 95.00

A. Somasundaram

*Future is in Our Hands 90.00

S. K. Sharma

*The Brilliance of Hinduism 95.00
*Sanskar Vidhi (Arya Samaj) 95.00

Dr. B.R. Kishore

*Hinduism 95.00
*Essence of Vedas 195.00
*Mahabharata 75.00
*Ramayana 75.00
*Supreme Mother Goddesses Durga (4 Colour Durga Chalisa) 95.00

Dr. Raj Bali Pandey

*Rigveda 75.00
*Samveda 75.00
*Yajurveda 75.00
*Atharvveda 75.00

Manan Sharma

*Buddhism (Teachings of Buddha) 95.00
*Universality of Buddha 95.00

Anurag Sharma

*Life Profile & Biography of Buddha 95.00
*Thus Spake Buddha 95.00

Udit Sharma

*Teaching & Philosophy of Buddha 95.00

Order books by V.P.P. Postage Rs. 20/- per book extra. Postage free on order of three or more books, Send Rs. 20/–in advance.

DIAMOND POCKET BOOKS (P) LTD.

X-30, Okhla Industrial Area, Phase-II, New Delhi-110020.
Phones : 41611861, Fax : (0091)-011- 41611866.
E-mail : sales@diamondpublication.com, Website : www.diamondpublication.com